FINANCIAL FREEDOM

Financial Freedom

BUILDING PERSONAL

WEALTH THROUGH

HOMEOWNERSHIP®

Ed Parcaut

BIG HANGRY
M E D I A

FINANCIAL FREEDOM

Building Personal Wealth through Homeownership

FIRST EDITION

ISBN   978-1-5445-3557-9 *Hardcover*
       978-1-5445-3558-6 *Paperback*
       978-1-5445-3559-3 *Ebook*

Contents

Introduction

This is the story about a $70,000 mistake.

Jeanette approached my firm one year ago. In her early thirties, she was newly divorced, with two kids living in Turlock, California. She found a home she wanted for $350,000. I worked out the numbers for her, and she was ready to make an offer. Then, a week later, one of my agents came into my office and said, "She changed her mind."

I reached out to Jeanette to understand why she no longer wanted the house. She explained that she was concerned about the monthly payment, which was higher than her current monthly rent payment. I realized she needed education on why it made sense for her to move forward with the house. I walked her through the benefits of purchasing right then, despite the slightly higher mortgage payment.

One of the most significant benefits was that her monthly payment would stay exactly the same for as long as she owned the house, unlike her rent payment, which would increase every year. In California, renters can see an increase in their rent of a half a percent every year to keep up with market rates. Her rent at that time was $1,900 a month. Every year, it would increase by $95. In contrast, her mortgage payment of $2,200 would stay the same for the entire 30-year mortgage.

Another benefit was that she was building equity in the home with each mortgage payment. House appreciation is currently seeing a 20 percent increase every year. I explained to Jeanette that she would be paying more for the same house by waiting a year. The $350,000 house would increase by $70,000 in a single year, resulting in her paying $420,000 instead of earning $70,000 in equity.

Homeownership would also benefit Jeanette by increasing her personal wealth, starting her on the journey to financial freedom. Even if she sold it in ten years, she would have enough equity in the house to put toward another home. Or she could keep it for the entirety of the mortgage and give her children generational wealth. After all, the average net worth for a home-owner is $200,000, while the average net worth for a renter is only $8,000.

Jeanette decided that, despite these benefits, she was not ready to purchase the home.

Recently, she reached out to me to inquire about purchasing that same home, which is now $420,000. The increase in appreciation had raised her payment by $200 to $2,400 a month. I walked her through the same benefits I had explained a year ago, but she decided to wait and save up more for the down payment (the increase of which would only save her $50 a month).

Since our last conversation, interest rates have increased by 1 percent. That translates to an additional $215 a month on the mortgage payment. Unfortunately, Jeanette is now priced out of the housing market in her area. If she wants to buy, she will have to move. For now, she is continuing to rent, but with continuous rent increases, it's likely she will soon be priced out of renting in the area as well.

What I could not get Jeanette to understand is that you are always at the right place in life to make the decision to purchase a home. You should never make your decision based on what the market and interest rates are doing.

THE FEAR OF HOMEBUYING

So many kids saw their parents lose their homes during the great recession in 2008–2012. As a result, they grew up thinking they shouldn't own a home because of what their parents experienced.

To make matters worse, these same kids, who are now young adults, keep hearing that a bubble is coming, which is a period where home values have increased so much that the demand is lost and values decrease.

No wonder they are hesitant to buy a home.

But a bubble is not coming. As I'm writing this book, less than a month of inventory is available to potential buyers. We're 4.3 million homes short of what is currently needed. To catch up, two million homes per year would need to be built for the next decade. And in 2022, we're on schedule to build only 1.2 million homes. It will take a while to catch up.

You should own a home. And, the moment you start thinking about buying a home is the best time to own one.

WHY NOW IS THE PERFECT TIME TO BUY A HOUSE

Affordability is close to the highest it's ever been, and it will only decrease over time for two reasons:

1. Housing prices will continue to rise due to lack of supply. As prices increase, houses become less affordable.
2. Interest rates are historically the lowest they've ever been. Although rates have risen since the pandemic, they are not close to rates we've seen in the past, which ranged from 6 to 13 percent. However, they will continue to rise.

Unless your income rises at the same rate as housing prices and interest rates, you will be squeezed out of the market. For example, if today you can afford a 1,500-square-foot home that costs $200,000, five years from now that same 1,500-square-foot home will no longer be affordable. Instead, for the same $200,000, you only will be able to afford a smaller house and one located in a less desirable neighborhood. Plus, because of rising interest rates, your mortgage payments will be several hundred dollars more per month than if you had purchased a house now instead of waiting.

When buying a home, mortgage payments are fixed. What you pay today will remain the same until you've paid off your mortgage, whether that's in ten, fifteen, or thirty years. Not only will your payment remain the same, but a part of each payment you make is applied to the principal. Over time you benefit by gaining additional equity in your home.

But that's not the only reason to buy now. For the past few years, housing prices nationwide have increased by 19 percent per year. You will benefit from that increase and any subsequent rise in prices.

You may be thinking that you'll just continue to rent if the housing market becomes unaffordable when you're ready to buy a house. But the supply for rental properties is just as bad as the supply for homes. In addition, rent payments will continue to rise forever, and renting does not enable you to build wealth. Once you stop renting, you own nothing.

When you buy a house, you're in the game, and you can use that equity to build personal or generational wealth.

Personal wealth gives you opportunities you would not have had otherwise, including generational wealth. With real estate, you have wealth to pass on to your children and your grandchildren. Even if you don't have children or don't plan to have children, personal wealth gives you the financial freedom to purchase other things.

For example, my wife and I bought a cabin in 2007 for $197,000. Eight years later, the cabin had appreciated to $450,000. We turned the equity into an additional thirty-two acres of land.

When you have equity, you can use it to:

- Improve the home you live in
- Buy your next home
- Take an equity loan and purchase a vacation home
- Purchase an investment property

Equity allows you to build passive income that you are not able to do any other way. At no other time in history have we seen so many people with this much equity available to them.

THE PROBLEM AND THE SOLUTION

Most people today are intimidated by the homebuying process. They don't understand how easy it is to go through the process of buying your first home. Instead, they assume it's too hard and they won't be able to do it.

This book will break down the homebuying process for you in a way that is easy to understand and nonintimidating. We'll look at the three most important factors that are considered when purchasing a home: income, assets, and credit. Understanding those three factors will allow you to understand where you are in the process, if you can buy a home right now, and when you will be able to buy if it's not now.

You'll also learn how important it is to build personal wealth and how purchasing your first home can help you build that wealth.

WHY ME?

I have been in the mortgage industry for twenty-five years. I began as a mortgage broker, before rising to management, and then starting my own mortgage company called Lending For Living. At my firm, I still help with origination, where I help buyers through the purchasing process. Origination includes reviewing applications, running credit, reviewing loan programs, examining assets and income, and creating the loan.

I love helping people, especially first-time buyers, through the origination process. It changes their lives forever. Studies show that children raised in a home that you own perform better in school and in life. Plus, once you own your own home, you never have to worry about someone telling you your payment is increasing at the end of the month. You can do whatever you want to your home: paint it, wallpaper it, change the flooring, etc.

You *own* it. There's no other feeling like that.

The look on the first-time homebuyer's face, whether they're twenty-two or fifty, never gets old. I get to help make dreams come true. Who doesn't want to help fulfill dreams all day long?

When I work with my clients, I always explain to them that if it's happened to you, it's happened to me. The 2008 downturn devastated a lot of homebuyers and ruined a lot of mortgage companies—including mine. The company I had at that time went under, and I had to claim bankruptcy. I had to rebuild, and I understand how difficult this process can be. I am here to help you move past your difficulties and begin the process of buying a home.

WHAT TO EXPECT FROM THIS BOOK

This book is a guide that will explain why it's important to buy your first home. I'll explain the various processes involved and the benefits you'll receive by going through each step.

Let's get started.

CHAPTER ONE

Understanding Credit

Vinnie, a young man in his mid-twenties, was ready to buy his first single-family home. His dad told him to listen to Real Estate Jerky, my radio show that helps listeners understand the homebuying process.

When Vinnie came to me, he thought he would have no trouble securing a loan. He thought he had a good credit score because one of the credit bureaus he watched showed he had a score of 650. Unfortunately, what Vinnie didn't know was that there are three different credit bureaus that each have their own score, and mortgage brokers take the middle of the three, not the average. His other two scores were 580 and 560, so we had to use the 580 score.

It's possible to get a loan with a score of 580. But because that's considered a poor score, it means he would have to incur a very high interest rate.

Vinnie, like most of my clients, wanted to get the lowest inter-est rate possible. To help Vinnie get his score up, I added his rental history to his credit report, which increased the score as he didn't have any late payments. Then, I had him get three secured credit cards, each with a $350 limit. With a secure credit card, you give the company the money for the balance you want (in this case $350), and that amount is now the limit on the card. If you give them $250, the limit is $250. On your credit report, they are considered the same as a regular credit card, even though they are secured.

Forty-five days later, Vinnie's score increased to 680. Once his score was elevated, we were able to finish the pre-approval, and he was able to purchase the house.

Unfortunately, Vinnie was not my only client to learn how your credit score could affect your interest rate—or how easily you could affect your score.

Jennie found out that you can damage your credit score by reviewing it too often. Jennie was in her early thirties, working for a big tech company. When Jennie came to me, she and her husband wanted to purchase their first home. They were looking for a single-family house that was big enough for them and their children. Her credit score was at 618, but I wanted her to increase it to 620 because even that small of a difference can affect your interest rates and loan amount.

I explained to Jennie that she needed to do two big things to improve her score. First, like Vinnie, we added on her rental payment history. Second, she needed to pay down some of her debt. She had several credit cards that were extremely close to their limit. The closer you are to your credit limit, the more it negatively affects your credit score. Ideally, you should be under 50 percent utilization of your credit cards at all times. If you can get down to a 10 percent utilization, you can get an even better rating.

However, during the process of improving her credit score, she decided to get her credit checked by someone else. Every time you have a hard credit check run, it takes points away from your credit scores. There is a small caveat to that: you have fourteen days after your initial credit check where you can have it reviewed by other people without it affecting your score more.

Jennie had her credit checked a second time thirty days after I initially checked it and while we were working to build it up. The result was that the points she was going to receive, she had now lost.

Once I explained to her what happened, she was on board with the plan and we were able to get those lost points back.

THE HISTORY OF CREDIT SCORES

FICO® is a scoring model that was originally developed by Fair Isaac Corporation, which was founded in 1956 by engineers and mathematicians Bill Fair and Early Isaac. In 1958, two years after their founding, they created the first credit scoring system.

This system was purchased by credit bureaus in 1981, before going public in 1987. Today, all three of the major credit bureaus—Experian, Equifax, and TransUnion—have their own proprietary scoring system. Experian uses Experience/FICO, Equifax uses Pinnacle Score (previously known as Beacon), and TransUnion uses Empirica. The term FICO was used in honor of the name of the original company, and because it's been around for a long time, it's still used today as a generic umbrella term, and often interchangeably with credit score. While the word FICO is still used, for the rest of the book, I'll use the term credit score to avoid any potential confusion.

WHAT'S A CREDIT SCORE?

A credit score is a history of how you utilize your credit. The score takes into consideration:

- If you pay your bills on time
- How close to the limit your credit cards are
- How much actual credit you have
- How long you've had credit cards
- How many installment loans you have
- How many times you've had your credit checked

At no other time in history has your credit score been so important. The reason is because your credit score tells mortgage brokers:

- If you qualify for a loan
- How large a loan you can get
- Your interest rate

A high credit score provides you with a lower interest rate and lower monthly payment, as well as giving you a wider range of loan programs to choose from.

During the Great Recession, three quarters of loans provided had a credit score of 640 or lower. Today, three-quarters of loans have a score of 740 or higher. Today, people have learned how to use their credit and how important it is, especially to homebuying.

Many people have a low credit score because they pay cash instead of buying on credit. If you have a low credit score, 580 or lower, you can get a loan, but it will need to be manually underwritten, and 95 percent of mortgage companies won't manually underwrite. The majority of mortgage companies will only perform automated underwrites.

The good news is that if you have been paying cash and don't have a high credit score, there are ways to build it up.

HOW YOUR CREDIT SCORE IS DETERMINED

The most common question I get about credit scores is how is it calculated?

- Payment history: 35 percent
- How much you owe: 30 percent
- Length of credit history: 15 percent
- Credit mix: 10 percent
- How much new credit: 10 percent

Payment history looks at whether or not you have late payments, charge-off debt, collections, and bankruptcy fees, all of which can affect your score.

Amount owed looks at how close your credit cards are to their limit. My firm says you should be at 50 percent utilization, but many credit bureaus and companies prefer you to be at 30 or even 10 percent. If you don't need to carry a balance on your card, find out when your credit card reports to the bureaus and pay it off in full the day before. This ensures you never show a balance on your score. However, creditors don't see that as a zero balance—they see it as the card not being active. They'll assign an inactive status for that card, which could either get you no credit or even give you a negative credit.

Credit history depends on how long you've had a credit card open. I ran a credit score for a friend who said her credit score would be 785. When I ran the report, it showed 690. She had a credit card for almost fifteen years that she had consistently paid on time, but she recently decided to cancel it. When you cancel your credit card, you lose all the history from that card. When you get a credit card, you never want to cancel it. Keep it, and keep utilizing it (put your weekly coffee on it, for instance) and then pay it off each month.

Credit mix is the combination of your loans, such as a car loan, credit cards, and mortgage.

For most people in their twenties and thirties, length of credit history is going to be a problem, because they've only had their credit for a short period of time. To fix that issue, we add secure credit cards and add your renting history. This will give you both more credit and improve your history.

These factors change daily. Every time you use your credit, it gets reported. Your credit score is a time in history at the moment your score is pulled. It could change ten minutes later, or it can change the next day. However, when we run your credit and see your score, that score can be used for your loan for up to 120 days, even if it changes tomorrow or thirty days from now.

If your car needs repairs during the 120-day period and you have to put $3,000 on your credit card, that won't affect your loan. The exception is if you get new credit. If you go to a department store during the 120 days and apply for a new credit card, it will put an inquiry on your credit, which could be an issue.

The same principle applies to buying a new car. If you buy a new car during the homebuying process, you've just killed your loan because you've drastically changed your debt-to-income ratio.

CREDIT REPORT RED FLAGS

When your credit report is run, be sure to review it carefully and look for red flags. The first thing you want to check is that all of your personal information is correct. For example, look at your list of past addresses and make sure there are no addresses listed that aren't yours. If there are, it could mean that someone was trying to steal your identity or attempt fraud. Make sure to report any address inaccuracies right away.

Second, check your derogatory marks, meaning check that any bad credit on your report is actually *your* bad credit. As an example, if you filed for bankruptcy, check that the bankruptcy information is accurate. Often when you file, the credit cards that were included in your bankruptcy are paid, but they don't get updated on your credit report. If you find something outdated or incorrect, contact the credit agency to have it fixed.

Next, check your late payments and any other items that are

showing under the derogatory category of your credit report. Is anything inaccurate? Again, if it is, contact the agency and get it fixed.

Then, look at the utilization of your credit. Make sure your balances are no more than 50 percent of your limits, but know that 30 percent is better and 10 percent is best. If your utilization is higher, work to decrease it, but you don't want a zero balance to show on your report.

Lastly, ensure that everything that you have paid on time is showing as paid on time.

Go through every line on your report and verify that it's correct. If not, dispute it and make sure it gets corrected.

CREDIT SCORE RANGES

Credit scores can range from 300 to 850. According to TransUnion, credit scores break down into the following categories:

- Poor: 300–590
- Fair: 580–670
- Good: 670–740
- Very Good: 740–800
- Exceptional: 800–850

However, my firm uses the following categories because these scores are where interest rates change for different loan programs.

- Fair credit: 640 and below
- Good: 680
- Great: 720
- Excellent: 760 and above

To get the best rate possible, you need at least a 760 credit score.

During the pandemic, lenders raised the minimum credit score on loan programs because a person with a 645 score is approximately seventeen times more likely to foreclose on a house than a person with a 745 score. It's important to get your score as high as possible before applying for a loan, so you can get a good interest rate and lower monthly payment.

ALGORITHM DIFFERENCES

When I run clients' credit, I often hear that they got a higher score from their app, such as Experian or Credit Karma.

However, mortgage companies use a different algorithm than what other companies use. When you get your credit run for a car loan, they'll see six different scores. When mortgage brokers run your score, we get three.

Credit Karma will show you a different score than the mortgage industry because they use a different algorithm. While this can be frustrating, the important thing is that you watch your score. It doesn't matter what app you use to watch it—just monitor it and constantly try to improve it.

If Credit Karma shows that your score goes down, investigate why and fix it. While these apps may not be accurate to what your mortgage broker sees, they can still help you stay on top of your score so you don't get blindsided by any issues once you go to purchase a home.

While there's always some variability, I've found that the scores mortgage companies pull are typically either exactly the same or, more often, lower than what your app is showing you. Focus on getting your score as high as possible in the app so that even if it shows lower with the lender, you are still in a great position.

Vantage score is a new score that uses the average of all of your credit scores, instead of just using the middle number as we currently do. This is not a good number for many people. If your three scores are 580, 660, and 670, and those are averaged, you'll end up with a score of 637, instead of being able to use the 660 score.

HOW NOT TO BUILD YOUR CREDIT SCORE

Experian Boost® is currently popular. Boost adds your utilities and other payments onto your credit report, which can increase your credit score. The current FICO score model that lenders use, however, does not take advantage of boost.

There are downsides to the practice of using boost. If you don't pay your utilities on time, it will affect your credit, whereas prior to adding the utilities to your credit score, utilities did not affect your credit (unless you reached a point where you defaulted on that bill and it went to collections).

In my opinion, if enough people begin adding utilities and other payments to their credit score, eventually credit companies will add them permanently to everyone's credit reports, which could be very detrimental to those who have issues paying bills on time. Adding utilities and other payments to your credit report will add seventeen points to your score (if you are very lucky), but there are better ways to increase your score without adding more debt to it. I recommend to all of my clients to not add a boost on their credit report.

Say you add your cable bill to your report and it increases your score for a few months. Then, for some reason, you are late paying one month. Because that bill is now on your credit report, it will affect your credit score both immediately and for a period of time afterward until that late payment falls off of your report. By not adding that cable bill to your credit report, the worst that happens because of a late payment is that you have to pay a small late fee. Your credit score is unaffected.

CHAPTER TWO

Income and Budget

Debbie and her husband had been missionaries for over twenty years. When they finally settled down in the United States, they moved to Manteca, California, where they both worked minimum wage jobs.

Debbie and her husband were in their mid-fifties and were ready to purchase their first home. They had been living in a trailer on her brother's property for three years, and they wanted their own property. They wouldn't be able to afford a home with their current salaries, so they lived on this property while Debbie went back to school.

She only had two years left on her bachelor's degree. Once she finished, she took a job at Amazon and increased her salary to $75,000 a year. Her husband was also able to find a better-paying job and increased his salary to $40,000. Now they were making a combined income of over $100,000.

Debbie was a longtime listener of my radio show, and when they were ready to start the homebuying process, she gave me a call (and was surprised to find that I answered all my own calls). She wanted to know how much they could afford. I took her basic information, ran their credit, looked at their income, and found that they could afford a home over $500,000.

Thanks to their increased salaries and minimal amount of debt, they were able to get a VA loan, a program that lets Veterans purchase homes with no money down.

They now live in their $475,000, three-bedroom, two-bath home. They could not believe that they finally owned their own home, even when the keys were in hand. I called them as soon as they closed to tell them congratulations, and she admitted to me that they thought owning a home was never going to happen. They were ecstatic walking into that front door.

GROSS VS. NET INCOME: WHAT'S THE DIFFERENCE?

Gross income is the actual dollar amount you are paid before taxes or deductions are removed. Your net income is what your pay is after taxes and deductions are removed.

If your salary is $78,000 a year, $78,000 is your gross income, while your net income will be around $58,300 (depending on your federal and state income tax bracket). However, your net income will fluctuate depending on what deductions are removed from your pay. These can include:

- Your state's income tax
- Federal income tax
- Social Security and Medicare taxes
- Health insurance

- Life insurance
- Distributions from your IRA
- Distributions from your 401k or 403b
- Payments to 401k or 403b loan
- Child support payments
- Alimony payments

The good news is that mortgage brokers don't care about your net pay. We look at your gross monthly pay and subtract any current 401k or 403b loan payments. The resulting number is the income we use to qualify you for your loan. Once we know your monthly income, we use it in a formula to calculate your debt-to-income ratio (which is discussed later in this chapter).

This monthly income is also used to calculate your budget.

CALCULATING BUDGET

Knowing your monthly budget is an essential part of qualifying for a mortgage. If you don't know what you can realistically afford, you could end up house poor, meaning that you have a house but you can't afford to eat, have a child, vacation, etc. You need to make sure the house payment works within your budget so you can still afford both basic essentials (food) and future wants (children or pets).

There is good news, however, if you want more house than you can afford on your current monthly income. At no other time in history have there been 11 million jobs vacant. You can get a different job, move into a different industry, or work at a different company in order to make more money so you can afford the home you want.

If you want or need a better job, but you don't feel qualified, there are several options available to you. You can go back to school. Or you can join a training program to go into a different field in your industry. For instance, if you're currently a medical assistant, you can get training to become an LVN nurse. Many companies are also currently increasing their base pay. Walmart, for example, is now paying $20 an hour for several positions that used to start at $15 an hour.

There are also companies willing to pay you to go to school to help you gain the qualifications needed for the next-level position, such as Amazon and Starbucks. So many companies are willing to help you grow as an employee to better yourself, enabling you to purchase your own home.

Once you know how much money you are making, the next step is to look at your expenses.

Do you have a car? If so, you need to consider more than just your car payment. You also need to include your car insurance payment as well as how much you spend on gas every month. Include your current rent payment. Next, add in your utilities: electrical, gas, water, cell phone, cable, and/or internet. Then, add in your grocery, takeout, and clothing expenses.

If you have a pet, include how much you spend on them, such as vet bills, pet insurance, food, toys, and doggy daycare. Next, add in your entertainment expenses, such as streaming service subscriptions, movie theater trips, or concerts. Lastly, add in your credit card payments. Create two options for this. Option one would be the minimum payment amount, while option two would look at how much you need to pay each month in order to pay that card off within three years.

Once you add all monthly expenses to your budget, look at how much money you have left at the end of the month. If your rent is $1,000 a month and your budget shows no leftover money, it may not be the best time to purchase a home. You may want to focus on building your income first or paying down your debt to free up more income. However, when you pay off a credit card, do not close it in order to protect your credit score, as discussed in Chapter 1.

Your budget will tell you if you have enough money to survive and grow. While it is possible to tighten your budget in some places, it's inadvisable to try and purchase a home on a budget with zero flexibility.

To figure out what you can afford, calculate 35 percent of what your gross pay is. That is the max amount you can spend on a mortgage payment, including taxes, insurance, and fees. If your gross pay is $6,500 a month, you can have a maximum house payment of $2,275. If that amount works in your budget and there are homes in the area available for that amount, that's great. However, if you cannot afford that amount or the houses in your area have a minimum house payment of $2,700 or $3,000 because of their size or value, then you have to start considering your options.

You can pay down your debt, you can increase your income, or we can potentially review different loan programs and costs based on down payment amounts. Realistically, though, if you are in an area where houses are around $300,000, you will need at least $1,800 a month for the payment. Where you are located will be a large factor in how much homes around you are worth. For instance, if you are in San Diego, entry-level homes run $800,000–$1,000,000, while in the Bay area it costs over $1,000,000 for a rundown entry-level home.

Don't be discouraged. You may need to move to buy your first home. I had a client who lived in Austin, Texas, which used to be an artist community and very affordable. Now, to live in the city costs at least $1,200,000. If you move twenty to thirty miles outside of the city, however, homes start to decrease in price to a more affordable range. This increase in pricing has happened with most of the major cities in the United States. Homes in Philadelphia, for example, have doubled in price over the last twenty years.

Setting up your budget will tell you how much you can qualify for. It can also help you understand where you are wasting money that could be spent more wisely. If you look at your budget and you're spending $1,000 a month on takeout and coffee, you can reduce that amount and instead use that income toward paying down credit card debt. That will help increase your credit score and free up money in your budget.

If you can take six months to pay off your credit cards, you won't care that house values have gone up 1.5 percent per month during that time. Why? Because there is nothing worse than having a house payment that doesn't allow you to pay off your credit cards. That path leads to more debt.

Your budget is the first step. It enables you to look at where you are today and where you need to make changes. Most people don't want to take this step because then they have to face the reality of where they're spending their money. This step is about growing up, facing how you have been living, and committing to change in order to build your life. Your budget enables you to create a plan by putting your numbers in perspective.

When calculating your debt, don't forget about your student loans, even if you are in deferment or forbearance. If you have a student loan and you aren't making a minimum payment every month, mortgage brokers are required to factor in at least half a percent of the total balance of the loan.

If you have a $3,000 balance, half a percent would be $15. That's not a problem. However, most people have multiple loans. If you have a $20,000 loan and a $35,000 loan that you aren't paying minimum payments on, your lender will have to factor in payments of $100 and $175, respectively, because we have to work under the assumption that you will eventually begin to pay the loans back. If we don't factor that amount in and you purchase a more expensive home, when you do begin payments again, you may not have enough money to handle both expenses.

This principle also applies to any nonmedical collections that show on your credit report. If you have $5,000 overall collection accounts that are not medical expenses, then lenders have to factor in a 5 percent payment of that amount. In this case, that would be $250 a month.

Child support and alimony can either be income or debt depending on whether you are receiving or paying it. While considering child support and alimony as income for the receiver is helpful, considering it as debt for the payer—the current model with all lenders—is an outdated method that should be changed. Why? If you were still married and living in the same household, you would be spending that money as part of your disposable income, not as debt. However, once it's considered child support or alimony, those funds become categorized as debt, putting it in the same category as a car or student loan.

For example, if your gross monthly income is $10,000 and you pay $2,000 in child support, that amount is shown as a debt against it. $2,000 becomes 20 percent of your debt-to-income ratio. This can hurt a person's chances at buying a home who would normally be able to afford that home, all because they pay child support and alimony. While they should be paying these to the appropriate party, the way it's classified should be changed, so it doesn't negatively affect the payer's financial situation.

Knowing your budget is essential, but mortgage brokers do not use your budget for qualifying purposes. The only information we use when determining if you qualify for a mortgage is the liabilities on your credit report, which we discussed in Chapter 1.

The budget is a guideline for you to know if you will be able to have a life once you buy your home—or sometimes even know if you are already living outside of your means. It helps you save money and focus on your future.

If your budget shows you can't afford the amount for the house you want, you can either get a better job or purchase the house you can afford. Then, you can either live in that house, build up equity and savings, and then sell it to buy a larger home, or you can rent it out, still build equity, and supplement your income with passive income from the rent payments.

EMPLOYMENT QUALIFICATIONS

When qualifying for a mortgage, you must be able to show two years of employment history where you were actively employed without any gaps. Those two years do not have to be at the same job or in the same industry. If you were a general laborer for company A, then a receptionist for Company B, and are now working in accounts payable for Company C, that is still considered working for two years.

Mortgage brokers do not look at job titles. We look at how you are paid: if you are an employee or an independent contractor.

This two-year rule can sometimes be complicated. If you've been an employee at a company for five years, but in the last six months, you start receiving overtime, commissions, or bonuses, you now have to have a two-year history of that extra pay. If you start to receive overtime, you must have a two-year history of receiving overtime. Or, in either case, your employer has to guarantee that you are going to receive that amount every month, which most employers will not do. However, if your company will guarantee that you will receive a specific amount of extra pay every month, that amount can be used as part of your total income.

I had a gentleman come in recently, sent to me from a real estate agent who wanted to see if I could qualify him for a larger amount. He was currently qualified for $350,000. However, he had qualified himself through an app. While filling out the application on that app, he put in the total income he was receiving from the company he had been working for as a wage earner. The catch was that he had started receiving overtime in the last four months, which he had never received before. He included his overtime pay in his income, which is how he was able to qualify for $350,000.

Once I reviewed his numbers, I realized he did not have a two-year history of overtime. Based on mortgage industry requirements, we could not use that extra income to qualify him. At that point, he only qualified for $210,000.

> It's not only important that you understand how to qualify for a mortgage, but that you go to the right people who can explain your specific situation. This book is an excellent resource for understanding the homebuying process, but this industry changes constantly. Sometimes that change is helpful for buyers, and sometimes it is not. Work with an expert who knows the most current changes and how best to help you purchase your first home.

Self-employed workers have different qualifications to meet. Being self-employed means that you get paid a 1099 or that you own 10 percent or more of a company. In this case, mortgage brokers must look at your tax returns to see how much income you are receiving on your personal income tax.

A common issue that I run into is when a self-employed person tells me that they make $200,000 a year, because that's what their company makes. Then, they write off all of their business expenses and have a bottom line of $30,000 that they claim on their personal tax return. That is the income we use when qualifying you.

We look at your business tax return and look for depreciation or anything we can add back into your lower income number. It is, however, an involved process. Because most business owners don't like paying taxes, they show the minimum income they can show on their tax return, which makes it very difficult for them to qualify for the home they want and can technically afford.

I worked with a farmer recently who only showed $25,000 of income on his tax return. However, when I put it into my system and added back in depreciation, he's now averaging $145,000 a year. Mortgage brokers look at the business and the person, but it is an involved process with many potential pitfalls.

Another example is from an architect. This architect had been self-employed for over a decade when he came to me to qualify for a home. Unfortunately, because he did not want to show income and pay taxes, his tax return only showed $15,000 a year. Once I added in everything I could, he was still only showing $22,000 a year, which is not enough to qualify for a home at all, let alone the one he was interested in.

There was a viable work-around, however. I told him that if he went to work for a firm that would utilize him as an architect, I could use that income right away because there wouldn't be a gap in his employment (remember the two-year rule). Thankfully, there were a few companies that had already approached him about joining their company. He negotiated with one of them, and started working with them the following week with an income of $120,000 a year. Once he received his first paycheck, I was able to use that income to help him qualify for and buy the home. He was able to close thirty days later.

There are also options if you show no income. Another gentleman client was in the process of buying a large home. He was in the construction industry and owned a company that builds large, multifamily buildings. He made over $2 million in 2020 alone. However, because he's able to offset income now for future jobs due to the tax code, his tax returns show zero income. In his situation, he couldn't afford a home according to his tax returns.

For him, I was able to use a bank statement loan. This enabled me to take all the deposits his company made in the last twenty-four months, divide it by twenty-four, and use that number as his monthly income. The result was that he now showed as making $3 million a month instead of $0 a month. However, requirements state that we can only take a portion of that $3 million and use it as income, typically between 50 and 80 percent, depending on the industry and ownership in which the individual is working.

This is just one example of a program you can use if you are self-employed if your income is offset due to your tax class.

The catch is that you cannot utilize cash. Banks and the federal government are adamant about knowing where cash comes from, thanks to the Anti-Money Laundering Act of 2020. Any cash deposits must be in your account for sixty days before we can utilize it. If you deposit $30,000 cash into your bank account, we have to prove where it came from or wait until it no longer shows as a deposit on your bank statements, which takes two months.

DEBT-TO-INCOME RATIO

Your debt-to-income (DTI) ratio (front/back) is essentially calculating for every dollar you bring in, how many cents of that dollar go toward just your mortgage payment, and how many cents go toward your mortgage payment and other debt.

Different loan programs will use different debt-to-income ratio calculations. Two common standards are 36 and 38, which means that either 36 cents of every dollar can go to your mortgage payment and other debt or 38 cents of every dollar can go to your mortgage payment and other debt. However, with different programs, that standard can be higher, such as 45 or even 56.

What DTI ratio you need depends on your budget, your loan program, and your income, and it is calculated automatically for lenders. If your loan program has a DTI of 41 and your monthly income is $6,500, your max mortgage payment would be $2,665 a month IF you have no other debt. Any additional debt you have would have to be taken out of that $2,665 amount. So if you have $500 in credit card payments and a $300 car payment, your max mortgage payment would be $1,865.

However, even if you have no other debt, you cannot increase your program's max DTI. If your program has a 41 DTI, even if you have no other debt, you can only use that 41 DTI calculation.

This number is important because it ensures you can afford to live. Lenders want to ensure that you can pay your house payment and other debt without defaulting on your loan.

If you default on your loan, the lender can repossess it. Defaulting means you have not made your house payment for a certain amount of time, usually ninety days. After that period, the lender can start foreclosure proceedings and kick you out of your house. Depending on the loan, you then have to wait a certain amount of time before you can buy another home, such as two or four years.

This is why it is so important to work with a professional, and why you need to know your credit score. Lenders will use your credit score and your DTI to understand how likely you are to default on your loan. The more likely you are to default, the riskier your loan is considered, and the higher your interest rate will be.

When you work with a professional, we work with you to understand your budget, your income, and your credit score so we can help pick the best program for you. We can also help you understand what assets you can—and cannot—use as collateral or for a down payment.

CHAPTER THREE

Assets

TIM'S CASH PROBLEM

My client, Tim, worked in construction, driving heavy machinery for several companies that all paid him an hourly wage. Together with his fiancé, he wanted to buy the house he was currently living in, a gorgeous single-family home, for $280,000.

However, because Tim was ambitious and because of the demand for his occupation, he was also hired for side jobs, making money that had nothing to do with his regular wage income. These side jobs, such as taking down trees, cleaning out fields, and making roads, were paid for by cash or check.

When Tim came to me, he told me he wanted to use the money from his side jobs to pay for the house he wanted to buy. I explained that he couldn't just deposit the checks into his account and use it for the home. Like most of my clients, Tim was shocked when he found this out. I've had several clients who sell their car, take the proceeds, deposit it into their bank account, and believe they can use that money for a down payment and closing costs. In their mind, it's their money, so why can't they use it?

Unfortunately, that is no longer a possibility. There's no trust in the lending industry anymore. Gone are the days of *It's a Wonderful Life*, when all you needed was a firm handshake. After the 2006 downturn, too many people lost their homes, and many mortgage companies went bankrupt. Today, we have to verify, verify, and verify everything.

The mortgage company has to know where each deposit came from when purchasing a house due to the Anti-Money Laundering Act. True to its name, this act is the government's way of ensuring you are not laundering money.

While Tim was initially discouraged—he wanted to use that money right away—we were able to put a plan together. The money Tim had been depositing in his account would, after sixty days, become seasoned, meaning you are to count that money toward assets. After two bank statements that show no deposits, that was his money, and I could utilize that income to help him purchase his home. However, if he deposited $5,000 into the account during the mortgage process, I would not be able to use that money because I would not be able to source it. I need to know who it came from and why the money was received to use a recent deposit.

If you want to purchase a house and you need to deposit cash, you can get gift money from your family. We'll talk about that later in this chapter.

I'm delighted to report that Tim and his fiancé have since closed on their home and are excited to start their journey with their newfound financial freedom.

BANK ACCOUNTS

Your bank account is always the first asset mortgage brokers review. This includes savings accounts, checking accounts, money markets, etc. We review your last two bank statements and use the amount shown on the most recent statement. The reason we look at the last two months' statements is to ensure that your money has been in your account for at least sixty days.

For instance, if you provide March and April statements, we use the balance shown on the April statement as your asset amount. If your March statement shows $8,000 and your April statement shows $6,000, we will use the $6,000 as your asset, because we know you've used up $2,000 of that money. However, if your March statement shows $3,200 and your April statement shows $10,000, your lender needs to know where that money came from.

If you received that money as a bonus for work, for instance, then we can easily trace where that money came from and it is usable. If that money was a cash deposit, we cannot use it until it's been in your account for at least sixty days. All money deposited into your account must be sourced and seasoned, meaning we have to be able to source it or wait for it to be seasoned.

The best rule of thumb is to talk to your mortgage broker before you deposit any money, whether it's cash or a gift from family or friends. They'll be able to walk you through the easiest way to get that money into your account and use it for your down payment. Many loan programs prefer that gift money be wired directly into escrow, along with a gift letter explaining where it came from. (We'll talk more about gift money later in this chapter.)

ESCROW

Escrow is a neutral party that makes sure that the original person gets their money, the loans associated with the property get paid off, and all the costs are taken care of correctly, so that when the process is finished, you have the right loan on your property and the person who owned it before is completely paid off.

An escrow account is opened either by your title company or an escrow company (your mortgage broker will ensure that you have one) as soon as the home is under contract. Once the account is opened, you can wire money for the down payment and closing costs directly into this account. Any gift funds or retirement account funds should also be wired directly into this account. By sending money directly into the escrow account, that money is considered sourced and seasoned (meaning there are fewer hoops for you to jump through to use it).

RETIREMENT ACCOUNTS

There are three types of retirement accounts you can sometimes use as assets: 401k, 403b, and some IRAs.

Regardless of which type of retirement account you want to use as an asset, be sure to consult your tax advisor first as there may be tax implications you should be aware of. At time of writing, you can take $10,000 out of your fund for homebuying costs before you get penalized, but that can vary depending on the loan type, retirement fund, and current laws.

Many retirement funds also offer the option of either taking the money out permanently or taking a loan against your fund and then paying yourself back over time. Remember this payment will be just like a car loan when calculating your debt-to-income ratios. Again, it depends on your specific fund's policies. All your mortgage broker cares about is that they know where the money is coming from and that it can be deposited directly into your escrow account. Unfortunately, some funds won't let you deposit directly into escrow, but that doesn't mean the money is not usable. It will just take more steps and verification before it can be used.

If you are going to take more than $10,000 out of your retirement account instead of doing a loan, be sure that it gets taxed correctly. I had one client who took $150,000 out of their 403b to buy their home and only had 10 percent taken out of that for taxes. However, because of the tax bracket they were in, that was not enough to cover all of their taxes and they had to pay more taxes the following April. The moral of the story is to make sure your lump sum is taxed at your actual tax rate, not at a generic 10 percent rate, or you may have to pay more later.

Some retirement accounts are considered public accounts and cannot be borrowed against or have money withdrawn. These include PERS (Public Employees' Retirement System) and SERS (School Employees' Retirement System), though there may be others. Again, be sure to check with your retirement plan administrator to see what restrictions your fund may have.

There are also some insurance policies that have a cash equity component. That can be considered an asset if you can take the money out. Your car, however, does not count as an asset.

If you can't borrow against it or take money out of it, it is not considered an asset.

GIFTING ASSETS

If you don't have assets, they can be gifted from your family in a few different ways.

One way is by gifting your down payment and closing cost money. They wire it directly into escrow and fill out a gift letter saying they're gifting you X amount of money. Most of the time, they do not need to prove where the funds came from so long as it is put directly into escrow and they write the gift letter, but be sure to check with your lender as policies can change quickly in this industry. This gift money is not considered a taxable event because it goes against your inheritance according to IRS rules. You can fill out an IRS Form 907 to declare that gift against your inheritance.

Another way is if you want to purchase a home your family owns. They can gift you equity in that house for you to buy the house from them. For example, if the house is worth $300,000, they can let you purchase the house for $250,000 and gift you the other $50,000 as equity for your down payment and closing costs. They receive $250,000 from the house and you don't have to pay out of pocket for the down payment and closing costs. In this situation, just like in the previous paragraph, fill out IRS Form 907.

It's important to note, however, that this gift will come out of the max amount of money your parents are allowed to gift you as nontaxable money over the life of their estate. At the current time of writing, this amount is $6 million. So if they gift you $50,000 in equity, you will only be able to receive an additional $5,950,000 over the rest of the life of the estate.

If you don't have the money right now, you can still buy a home if you have income and credit or some way to get the down payment and closing costs, such as from a retirement account or gift money. Don't lose hope just because you don't have the cash right now.

Many parents will help their children. I told my own children that I won't pay for their wedding, but I'll gladly give them money for a down payment on their first home. Why waste $50,000 on a single day that will only provide you with memories when you can use that money to start building your own personal wealth? A wedding is a few hours of a single day. A home changes everything, because you then have an asset that helps you your entire life.

The loan you get to buy your home, however, will vary depending on your specific situation.

CHAPTER FOUR

Loan Programs and Interest Rates

It's 1932. Norman and Virginia Smith just bought their first home. They were in the 10 percent of people who were able to buy a home. (90 percent of families rented in the 1930s.) The Smiths had to give the bank 50 percent for the down payment—a little over $2,500—which was almost all their savings.

A year later, there was a run on their bank (think that scene in *It's a Wonderful Life* when all the townspeople demanded their money from George Bailey). The bank needed money to give people, so they demanded the Smiths pay off the rest of their loan immediately. Norman and Virginia had spent all their money on the down payment and couldn't pay the rest of the loan back, so the bank foreclosed on their home and kicked them out within the week.

You might be thinking, *Banks can't do that!* It's true that banks today can't, but in the early 1930s, they could. That's why in 1934 the federal government put together the Federal Housing Administration (FHA). The FHA was created to look at the banking system and regulate how the industry handled mortgages.

The FHA's goal was to both broaden the number of people who were able to obtain mortgages and make it safer for them to do so. Before the FHA, there was zero protection for homebuyers. Plus, having to put 50 percent down to buy a house was unrealistic for the vast majority of people at that time when wages were a dollar a day and homes were five thousand dollars. The FHA created loan programs that let potential homebuyers pay a smaller down payment. In essence, they created mortgage insurance.

Mortgage insurance is an added cost to your mortgage that is insurance for the lender in case you default on your loan by ensuring the lender is made whole. Mortgage insurance is helpful for everyone involved in the homebuying process. It helps borrowers by allowing a smaller down payment while also protecting the mortgage company from the higher risk of a smaller down payment.

Today, homeowners can put as little as 3.5 percent down using an FHA loan. That's a lot better than paying 50 percent down. Would you rather save $7,000 for a down payment on a $200,000 house or $100,000?

The FHA also ensured that banks could no longer call loans due at any time, creating additional protection for homebuyers. The FHA (now called HUD or the Department of Housing and Urban Development) created parameters that loans could only be called due and payable if you don't make a payment for ninety days.

After those ninety days, banks can create a notice of default, and then banks have to go through another 120 days of foreclosure processes before they can remove the homeowner from the house. Thanks to the FHA, if you make your payments on time, the bank cannot make your loan due and payable or foreclose on you.

If you have an FHA loan, the bank has to work with you and put together twelve months of home payments attached to the loan, a practice called partial pay of insurance. If we hit a bubble tomorrow and you had an FHA loan, you could miss up to twelve payments and the bank could not kick you out of the house. Instead, they have to do a partial pay, which means they apply that amount to the insurance, which is then attached to the house as a second loan. If at that time you start making house payments again, you can keep the house, and then, if you refinance or sell it down the road, you pay the missing payments.

Today, Norman and Virginia's great-granddaughter Debra and her husband Peter, have owned their own home for the past three years. They were able to purchase it with just 3.5 percent down using an FHA loan. Over those three years, they've been able to build over $100,000 in equity. Their home is the perfect size for them and their two children, but once their kids are out of the house, they'll be able to sell the home and purchase one that suits their new needs—and they'll have plenty of equity to do so.

Debra and Peter are part of the 65 percent of people in the U.S. who own a home today. That's six out of ten people who own a home today versus one out of ten in the 1930s. That's a big difference.

IT'S NOT YOUR RESPONSIBILITY

In this chapter, you'll learn about the most popular loan programs available. However, I want to make it very clear that it is *not* your responsibility to find the right loan program for you. It's your mortgage broker's responsibility, because every potential buyer's situation is different and there is constant change in the mortgage industry.

There are always new programs coming out and changes to old programs. What might be best for you today may not be best for you tomorrow. A loan program may have a minimum credit score of 640 today, and tomorrow it could be changed to 580.

Your mortgage broker's job is to look at your specific situation, look at the different loan programs available, and then find the best program to fit your specific situation. For example, if you want to buy a home in a rural area, your mortgage broker will want to look into a USDA loan first to see if you can buy with no money down. However, if you want to buy in a city, a USDA loan is off the table.

There is so much information around loan programs—information that's constantly changing—that the mortgage industry can't stay on top of it on a daily basis. We have to look into each program's specifics every time we have a new client.

If you try to rely on information you find on the internet, you may think you need a 20 percent down payment to buy a house, when really you only need 3 percent down—or even nothing down. The information readily available through a search engine is not always accurate.

There is nothing wrong with understanding the different programs available, but know that your lender will look at what the best program is for *you* specifically. Reading this book is just the first step. It will provide you with the knowledge to understand what's available so you can ask the right questions. The next step is to find someone to help you.

WHAT *IS* A LOAN PROGRAM?

A loan program is essentially a mortgage. The reason we call it a loan program instead is because each state has a different type of loan. In some states, they may be mortgages, while in others, such as California, they are called a trust deed, while in still others, it could be called a promissory note. Loan program is a generic umbrella term that helps ensure that everyone is on the same page regardless of where they live.

FHA LOAN PROGRAM

The FHA loan program is often referred to as for first-time homebuyers, but it really means that you don't have another home at the time that you are buying. Essentially, you cannot use an FHA loan for your vacation home. It is for primary residences only.

FHA loans only require 3.5 percent of the purchase price for the down payment, and it has a credit score allowance of 580–685 without a large difference in interest rates. This flexibility ensures that the FHA loan program can be used by a large number of people.

It's important to note that if you put less than 20 percent down, you will have mortgage insurance added. With FHA loans, your mortgage insurance will stay on your loan for the full life of the loan, with two exceptions. If you choose a 15-year loan or if you put 10 percent down, then the mortgage insurance will only be on there for eleven years.

The only caveat to the FHA program is that it has loan limits that are determined by county. This means that the amount of the loan has a limit depending on the average median income for that area.

For instance, in Stanislaus County in California, the max loan limit for an FHA loan is $460,250. However, in Tuolumne County, just a few minutes away, the max loan limit is $420,200. Every single county in the United States will have a different loan limit.

This number is calculated by HUD every year, usually in October–November, published in December, and put into effect on January 1 of the following year. Your mortgage broker will be able to tell you the limit for the area you are looking to purchase in, as an internet search may be out of date depending on when you are buying. If you are looking to purchase in a higher-priced area, the FHA loan limit may be less than what the houses are currently selling for. Because you won't be able to use the FHA loan, look into a conventional loan instead.

USDA LOAN PROGRAM

USDA is a zero down loan program for homes in rural areas. You can visit the USDA website at usda.gov (or contact your mortgage broker) to find which properties are eligible for this loan. By zero down, it means that this loan has 100 percent financing. However, because you are putting less than 20 percent down, you will have mortgage insurance.

Again, as this is a government-funded loan, they use the income of the area to calculate which areas are eligible for USDA loans.

There are two other eligibility components for this loan: income and debt-to-income ratio. When you go to their website, you can also put in your income to ensure that you don't exceed the limit for the area.

VA LOAN PROGRAM

The VA loan program was created originally for Veterans coming back from war to help them purchase a house, either a single-family home or up to four units (as long as you live full-time in one unit and qualify for the mortgage for the entire property). To qualify for the program, you must be either a Veteran or active duty. The VA loan program is 100 percent financing, meaning no money down, for qualified applicants.

Two years ago, the government changed the program to make it easier for people to purchase. Like FHA, it used to have county limits, but today it only has a maximum limit of $2.5 million that applies to the entire country.

However, even though the VA guarantees the loan, the program is done through lenders, and each lender may have their own maximum limit. Currently, that limit for the majority of lenders is between $1.5 and $2.5 million.

VA loans have fixed or adjustable rates (though most people

choose fixed), and can either be fifteen or thirty-year loans. You can easily refinance down the road because you've already qualified for the loan. Interest rates for VA loans are always lower than conventional or USDA loan rates, and are about the same as FHA.

The widow or widower of a Veteran who died can continue utilizing the program as long as they don't remarry and are receiving benefits.

CONVENTIONAL LOAN PROGRAMS

Conventional loan programs are for everyone. If you are paying less than 20 percent down, you will have mortgage insurance. However, eventually the mortgage insurance can be removed from your loan. Once you've paid the loan down to 80 percent of the LTV (loan to value), you can ask your lender to remove the insurance. While they don't have to at this point, once you are at 78 percent LTV, they have to remove the mortgage insurance.

For example, if your house was sold for $100,000, you would get a loan for $97,000 (because you paid 3 percent down). Once you pay your loan down to $80,000 (that's the 80 percent LTV amount), you can ask your lender to remove the mortgage insurance. If they don't, once you pay that loan down to $78,000, they have to remove the insurance. Once that mortgage insurance is removed, your monthly payment will decrease based on whatever the mortgage insurance amount is.

There is a conventional loan program for first-time homebuyers, which means you cannot have owned a home in the last three years. This program allows you to purchase with only 3 percent down.

There are other conventional loan programs available for home-buyers that require 5, 10, 15, or 20 percent down.

However, if you have 20 percent or more to put down on your loan, I would suggest you put less. I realize that sounds counter-productive, but let me explain. I recently ran two scenarios for a client. Having mortgage insurance added $78 to their monthly payment when they put 10 percent down. They wanted to know if they should put 20 percent down instead, which would mean paying an extra $30,000. I showed them that it would take them over 32 years to pay themselves back that $30,000 at $78 a month. That is longer than the life of their mortgage!

Instead, they could keep that $30,000 in the bank in case it is needed for life events. I've seen so many people put all of their cash down on their house and then, within a few months or years, they need some of it, so they come back to me for a refi-nance. Cash is opportunity. Don't use all of your cash on your down payment so you can save yourself the hassle of needing a refinancing.

REVERSE MORTGAGE LOAN PROGRAM

If you are sixty-two years or older, you may qualify for a reverse mortgage loan program. With this program, you do not make the interest payment on the loan. Instead, that interest payment is added to the principal of the loan.

For these older homeowners who don't want to move out of

their house but may need extra income for some reason, they can stay in their same house, refinance it with a reverse mortgage, and use the money they get to live on.

You can also use a reverse mortgage to purchase a home. For this type of loan program, you sell your existing home and, depending on your current age and how long you are estimated to live, you will put at least 50 percent of your proceeds from the sale toward the new home purchase. Then you never have to make another loan payment on that house until each person on the loan passes away. At that point, the heirs will take that loan and can either pay it off through a refinance or sell the property and take any proceeds that are left from the sale.

This program assumes that as the value of the house increases over time, the amount due on the loan won't exceed the value of the house at the end. The calculations can be complicated with this type of loan, however, so it's important to work with the right mortgage broker to be sure that it is the best decision for your situation.

If when the last person on the loan passes away, there is more owed on the house than it is worth, the property goes back to the bank. No heirs or family members are responsible for paying back the reverse mortgage. Heirs only get involved if there is equity left in the house.

NON-QM LOAN PROGRAMS

Non-QM loan programs are often called bank statement loans or self-employed loans. In 2008, when the government got involved in how mortgages were issued, they considered FHA,

VA, USDA, and conventional loan programs Qualified Mortgage Programs, or QMs. If you're not a part of any of these programs, you're considered non-QM, or non-Qualified Mortgage Programs.

These programs are anything that uses above-average interest rates or costs, and can be used for primary or non-primary residences. They are good for people who don't fit into the standard loan program because of their job or how they get paid. Essentially, they are alternative programs to the normal programs. They used to be called subprime mortgages (FHA, VA, USDA, and conventional programs are considered prime mortgages).

For non-QM programs, lenders look at the last twelve to twenty-four months of income that you deposited into your bank, average it, and use that average as your income per month. For example, if you are a self-employed individual and have $100,000 worth of deposits over twenty-four months, your monthly income will be $4,166 a month.

You may not be able to use a conventional loan program because you are new to being self-employed and don't have two full years of tax returns. Or you've been self-employed for two years, but you started in June and so you've only filed one full year of tax returns. Non-QM programs can be used to help you purchase a home as you can't use the normal programs without two years of tax returns.

I have one gentleman who works in manufacturing and wanted to purchase a house. However, because he is a manufacturer, the way he has to offset purchases means that his tax returns show he only makes $60,000 a year. The home he wanted to purchase was $1.5 million, so he didn't qualify using normal loan programs.

Instead, I looked at his business deposits for the last twenty-four months and averaged them. By using this method, his monthly income became $300,000 instead of the $5,000 his tax returns showed.

If you are not a wage earner, meaning you don't have a W-2, non-QM programs may be the best option for you. Often people who own their company have the cash to purchase a home, but they don't want to utilize it. That manufacturer gentleman had $2 million in cash that he could have used to purchase the property, but he wanted to save that cash to be able to invest it back into growing his company. Again, cash is opportunity, and he wanted to use it for future business projects.

Non-QM programs are also good for people who have a trust. If you have $500,000 in a trust and we can show that you can take that money out, we can divide that amount by a number of years (depending on your trust's rules and situation), and use that amount as income, something that cannot be done with normal loan programs.

Other non-QM programs include DSCR (debt service coverage ratio) loans, which can help you qualify for a loan without using your income (instead, you use the income of the rental property), and asset depletion mortgages, which look at the total amount of your assets, divide it by thirty-six months, and then decide if that's enough income to offset your mortgage payments and expenses.

SELLER FINANCING

There are some situations when you can opt for seller financing instead of a non-QM or prime mortgage. If you don't qualify for any of the other programs, you can ask the seller—if they own the house free and clear—to hold the note on the loan. This means that they act as the bank for the loan.

Often, when people are selling their house, they're going to put that money in the bank or other holding account, and they aren't going to receive any interest from it. These people are usually willing to carry the note.

This is often done when someone is purchasing vacant land. For vacant land purchase, you have to put 50 percent down and find a local bank to get your loan. The seller is often willing to accept a smaller down payment. For example, when my wife and I purchased thirty-two acres of land, we asked the seller if they would carry the note at 5 percent for the next five years and 20 percent down. This enabled us to be able to get a construction loan through a more traditional loan program.

With this type of financing, the seller is still attached to the property through the loan. If the buyer defaults, the seller keeps all of the money paid to them so far and they get the property back. The property does transfer ownership to the buyer, but the rules for the mortgage are the same as all the other loan programs, so both the buyer and seller are protected. You can also negotiate interest rates with the seller, though they'll generally want at or above current market rates.

HARD MONEY

Hard money is private money, meaning that an individual or private institution is lending money at 10 percent or greater interest rates. Hard money should always be a last resort for the majority of people.

House flippers often use private money because they can get the money they need to purchase a house within 24 to 48 hours. If you want to use hard money, you should still start with a mortgage broker. They can make sure it's the right decision.

CHOOSING THE RIGHT LOAN PROGRAM

Choosing the right loan program for you is extremely dependent on your personal situation, where you want to buy, your income, your debt amount, and your credit score, among other factors.

For instance, say you are a Veteran selling your old house, buying a new house, and you have 20 percent for a down payment. Most people think they wouldn't use a VA loan again, but because the interest rates are lower with VA loans, it is always better to choose it, no matter how much money you have to put down.

However, if you don't have access to the VA loan program, you have to look at more factors, such as what your credit score is. Someone with a 680 credit score and 5 percent down won't want to use a conventional loan, because conventional loans have much greater risk-based pricing. This means that every little thing that affects your credit score can have a big effect on your interest rate. If you don't have over a 700 credit score, you don't want to use a conventional loan at all.

Instead, you should choose an FHA loan because even though FHA also has risk-based pricing, your interest rate is not as affected. If you have a 685, your FHA interest rate could be 3.5 percent, whereas if you have a 625, your rate could be 3.75 percent. However, with a conventional loan, just a two-point difference in your credit score could be the difference between getting a loan at all and a much higher interest rate.

PURCHASING FOR YOUR KIDS

While most people are purchasing a single-family home, that's not your only option with most loan programs.

One of my agents, Amy, wanted to help her daughter buy a home in Tuolumne County. I told her about a type of FHA loan program that enables you to purchase a duplex, triplex, or fourplex (two units, three units, or four units, respectively) as long as the person buying it is living in one of the units. Then they can utilize the other units as rent toward their payment to qualify.

Amy helped her daughter buy the triplex with only 3.5 percent down, and her daughter lived in one of the units for a year and a half until she went back to school. They fixed up each of the units and began renting them out as well. By renting out all three units, they make $1,500 a month in profit.

After her daughter finished school, a year and a half later, she bought herself a single-family home and was able to put 10 percent down, thanks to saving money from her triplex. The mortgage on her new home is $2,000 a month, so she is able to use the $1,500 a month from her triplex profits and only pay $500 a month for her current mortgage.

Recently she contacted me to purchase another house to move into and put 10 percent down. She's keeping her current home to rent it out for $2,500 a month. At that point, she'll have $1,500 a month from the triplex and $2,500 a month from the first home, for a total of $4,000 a month that she can use to pay for all of the mortgages.

She's building her wealth through real estate, and she's doing it by putting down 10 percent instead of 20 to 25 percent like most people.

If you are not going to live in one of the units, you have to put 20 to 25 percent down, depending on whether it is two, three, or four units. If you are going to live there, you only have to put 3.5 percent down. So if you want to purchase a $400,000 property without living there, you'll have to put 25 percent down, which is $100,000. If you live there, however, you only have to put down $14,000.

With most loan programs of this type, you have to live in the unit for at least one year, but be sure to check with your lender to verify. This is a great option for younger people who don't have a family yet. You buy the property as your first property, and then you can live off of the rent you make from the other units.

OR FOR YOURSELF

A friend of mine and his wife recently purchased a duplex in San Clemente, California, which is just a block away from the beach. They used an FHA loan program, just like Amy and her daughter, and now they live on one side of the duplex and rent the other side out as an Airbnb. The rental profits pay for their entire mortgage.

Before purchasing their duplex, they owned two homes in Oakdale, California. They had both worked for the local school system, and while there, I helped them purchase the single-family home they lived in and another home to use as a rental. Both purchases were made in the late 2000s, around the time of the housing bubble, so they were very inexpensive. (In California at that time, home prices dropped around 50 percent.)

After three years of appreciation, they decided it was time to move to San Clemente in Southern California, a beach community they had always wanted to live in. However, the FHA limit in that area was $840,000, and the duplex was $950,000, meaning they had to put $110,000 down in order to qualify for the FHA loan. They sold both of their properties in Oakdale, and used those funds to pay for the duplex.

Today, their duplex is worth $1.9 million. Now that their kids are leaving for college, they are deciding what they want to do next. They could sell their duplex, but I am against selling a rental when it is making money. Why would you sell a rental and lose all of the potential income from renters as well as the appreciation of the property over time? Before you ever sell a rental property, be sure to consult your mortgage broker as well as a tax advisor so you understand all of the pros and cons.

Even if you want to sell a single-family home that you are living in and not renting, be sure to talk to your tax advisor. For a normal primary residence in the United States, there is a $250,000 deduction per individual who owns that home. So if you are married, you have a $500,000 maximum deduction. If you bought a home for $500,000 and it's appreciated to $1.3 million, you are going to pay capital gain taxes on the sale amount over the $500,000 in appreciation, which in this case is $300,000.

When I am working with my clients, I make sure they have a financial planner, tax advisor, and trust lawyer. If they don't, I help them get these people so that you make the best decision for your situation, whether you are buying or selling a home. If you are going to sell your home and you find out that you have to pay 22 percent on $300,000 worth of capital gains, you may want to take a different approach.

INTEREST RATES

I have never had a single person call me and say, "I want the highest rate and the most costs." Everyone wants the same thing: the lowest rate and the lowest costs. This is understandable, but you have to be careful because sometimes when you focus on this, it can be detrimental to what you're trying to do.

For instance, say you are trying to get a loan with the lowest interest rate. When I look at a loan, I factor in your credit score and LTV, put it in our system, and it gives me what rates are available for you.

The Impact of Rising Mortgage Rates

Monthly Mortgage Payment (Principal and Interest)

	MORTGAGE INTEREST RATE					
	6.00%	**5.75%**	**5.50%**	**5.25%**	**5.00%**	**4.75%**
$450,000	$2,698	$2,626	$2,555	$2,485	$2,415	$2,248
$425,000	$2,548	$2,481	$2,413	$2,347	$2,282	$2,217
$400,000	$2,398	$2,334	$2,271	$2,209	$2,147	$2,086
$375,000	$2,249	$2,189	$2,130	$2,071	$2,014	$1,957
$350,000	$2,099	$2,043	$1,988	$1,933	$1,879	$1,826

HOME LOAN AMOUNT

Principal and interest payments rounded to the nearest dollar. Total monthly payment may vary based on loan specifications such as property taxes, insurance, HOA dues, and other fees. Interest rates used here are for marketing purposes only. Consult your licensed mortgage advisor for current rates.

Interest rates are determined by your loan amount, loan program, credit score, and down payment. Your credit score will be the biggest determinant of your interest rate, then your LTV (or down payment), then your loan program, and then the property you are buying.

There are also outside forces that can affect your interest rate.

In the 1930s, when you walked into a bank to get a loan, the bank itself would lend the money. Today, the bank itself does not lend you the money. Since the early 2000s, the FHA, VA, and conventional loan companies have guaranteed the loan, and the money comes from the secondary market, also known as the mortgage-backed security market.

Essentially, your loan gets put into a group of loans that is then sold off to the secondary market. Interest rates are now based on mortgage-backed securities and how loans are sold on the secondary market. Interest rates can now change daily based on what is happening in the market: whether people are selling, whether people are buying stocks or bonds for protection, etc.

People commonly think the Fed affects their interest rates, because that's what they hear on TV. "The Fed met today and raised interest rates." "The Fed met this week and lowered interest rates." In reality, the Fed only affects the fed fund rate, which is what other rates are tied to, such as the prime rate (used for HELOCs or home equity lines of credit), car loans, and credit cards. It does not affect mortgage interest rates.

OUTSIDE FORCES THAT AFFECT INTEREST RATES

Whether people are investing in stocks or whether they are investing in bonds can affect interest rates. When the market goes down, people will quickly invest in bonds and mortgage-backed securities instead of stocks, which can lower interest rates—usually. We're in a special situation today where, even though people are doing a flight for safety to bonds, interest rates are increasing because the rate of inflation is too high.

Higher inflation rates can also drastically affect interest rates. The higher the inflation rate, the higher the interest rates. In June 2022, our inflation is close to 10 percent, which has increased interest rates to almost 6 percent. That feels high today, because we are coming out of a historic low for interest rates. In 2020, because money was being thrown into bonds thanks to the pandemic scare (causing rates to drop quickly), interest rates dropped to 2–3 percent, which was an amazing rate. Today, we are seeing double that rate, which has caused many potential buyers to hesitate before buying.

Despite an increase in interest rates, it's still a good time to buy. There have been huge improvements in the homebuying industry since Norman and Virginia bought their home. Today, both buyers and lenders are protected, and no matter what your situation, there's a program available to fit your needs.

However, there is more to buying a home than simply choosing the right loan program. You also need to understand the extra costs associated with it.

CHAPTER FIVE

Closing Costs and Prepaid Items

John and his wife were in their early thirties, ready to buy their first home. He reached out to me, and after getting all of their information together, I asked John how much they had for their down payment on the $500,000 home they were looking to purchase. He told me they had $35,000 set aside.

Unfortunately, John, like many first-time homebuyers, didn't know that he needed more than just a down payment. I explained to John and his wife that they also had to pay for closing costs, which includes fees for escrow, title, underwriting, applications, origination, processing, and more (all of which I'll explain later in this chapter). Your closing costs can range from 2–4 percent, depending on the home, location, and loan type.

John needed 5 percent for his down payment, per his loan program requirements, which totaled $25,000, while his closing costs came to $7,000. However, he also needed $3,000 to prepay his taxes and insurance. Thankfully, because John had

$35,000 set aside, he was able to meet his down payment minimum and pay the closing costs and prepaid items.

If John only had $25,000, I would have had to adjust his down payment amount to offset the money needed for closing costs. Another option would have been to ask the seller to pay the closing costs. In a seller's market, such as the one seen in the early 2020s, this is rarely able to be done, but in a buyer's market, it's a common request.

When the seller pays the closing costs, they still net the same dollar amount they wanted, while your closing costs are added to the purchase price, meaning it's a write-off for the seller and a write-off for you.

PREPAID COSTS

Often homebuyers will confuse prepaid costs with closing costs. Prepaid items include the property insurance, which must have one year paid up front, and property taxes, which are dependent on your state. Property taxes will need to be paid up front, however, that amount can vary depending again on your state's requirements and the time of year you are purchasing the house.

CLOSING COSTS

There are several parts to closing costs, some of which are dependent on the mortgage company, some on the escrow company, and some on attorneys.

MORTGAGE COMPANY COSTS

Before you close on your home, your mortgage broker will provide you with a loan estimate, which will list out (among other things) all of the closing costs: what they are for and how much they are.

Charges from your mortgage company can include:

- Origination charge: This is the fee from your lender for giving you the loan and creating the paperwork involved.
- Processing fee: The fee to process the loan.
- Underwriting fee: The fee to ensure the loan is valid and will be approved.
- Wire transfer fee: This fee only shows up if your lender charges for wire transfer, generally used in the case of gift money being put into your escrow account.
- Appraisal fee: The fee paid to the appraiser for appraising the house.
- Inspection fee: The fee paid to the appraiser to reinspect the property, if necessary.
- Credit report fee: The fee paid to run your credit report.
- Tax service fee: A closing cost that ensures the borrower pays their property taxes on time.
- Flood certification fee: An incurred fee to check if the property is in a flood zone.
- Recording fees: The fee you pay the local county to record the deed to trust (or the promissory note, depending on where you live).
- Transfer tax: The fee the government charges you to transfer the property to the next person.
- Mortgage insurance: Insurance to protect the lender in case you default on the loan.

- VA funding fee: Fee that is paid to the VA in case you default on the loan.
- USDA Loan Guarantee fee: Fee that is paid to USDA in case you default on the loan.
- Occasional small fees dependent on the county and state you are buying in.

All of the fees charged by the mortgage company are to pay them back for the cost of creating the mortgage. However, all of them—except for your mortgage insurance, VA funding fee, and USDA fee—are negotiable with your lender.

There can sometimes be a loan discount, which shows when you've bought your rate down. In layman's terms, this means you are paying to reduce your interest rate.

While this sounds great on the surface, there is a diminishing return on them, which means that paying too much for a lower interest rate will eventually not benefit you in the long run.

For instance, if you're saving $40 by lowering your interest rate, but it costs you $6,000, you should consider how long it would take you to pay yourself back that $6,000, which would be 150 months. Anything that would take you more than thirty-six months to pay yourself back is not worth paying for the lower rate. Instead, it would be cheaper to pay the higher interest rate over time.

There is also the option to raise your interest rate in order to get credits to help pay for some of your closing costs. All of these options can be, and should be, discussed with your mortgage broker.

ESCROW AND TITLE FEES

Depending on what state you are purchasing in, you will either have an escrow company or attorney who handles your escrow for you. Your escrow company is a neutral party who takes all of the money from both the buyer and seller, and makes sure that the correct amount goes to the correct party.

Regardless of who is handling the account, there will be a fee for both the buyer and seller. Your escrow company can charge fees for:

- Document prep
- Notary
- Attorney

Title insurance is a fee you pay in order to ensure that the home's title is free and clear of any encumbrances, i.e., that the only loan on that title is the loan you are putting on it. It protects you as the new owner and it protects the lender.

Title insurance essentially means that if Joe buys a house and, a few years down the road, it's discovered that there is an overdue loan from six years ago still on the house that the title insurance company missed, Joe is not obligated to pay that loan off. It also protects the lender for the same reason: they don't have to pay off the missed loan if title insurance was used.

If the title insurance company finds a lien or old loan on the home that should not be there, they will take the steps to have it removed before the purchase is completed, so neither the new owner nor the lender is on the hook. If they miss something that shows up years down the road, the title insurance company is responsible for that outdated loan or lien, instead of the owner or lender.

PROPERTY TAXES AND HOME INSURANCE

As discussed earlier, there are several prepaid items that must be paid at time of closing. This includes property taxes, which will vary depending on where you live and when you buy.

If you are buying your home in June and taxes were due in April, you may have to pay the seller back for the prepayment of the property taxes. Property taxes are paid to the county and vary by both state and county. Most of the time, these taxes are bundled into your mortgage payment, so it's important to discuss with your mortgage broker how they handle these taxes.

Most companies will have you put tax money into an impound account so that when your taxes are due, you have enough money in that account to pay the taxes, and then the taxes are paid by the mortgage company for you. This is a good thing for you because if you don't pay your property taxes after a set amount of time, usually at five years, then a lien can be put on your house and that property can be sold at a tax sale.

Home insurance is often handled the same way as your property taxes. Sometimes called hazard insurance or property insurance, this covers you in the event of damage to the house, such as a tree falls on it, it catches on fire, etc.

Say your home insurance costs $1,200 a year. One hundred dollars a month will be put into your impound or escrow account and paid to your insurance company on your behalf.

Having all of these costs bundled into your payment ensures that you don't have to worry about whether or not you can afford all of the external costs that come with having a home. It gives you a clear picture of what amount you will have to pay every month with no surprises, avoiding the worst-case scenario where you purchase a home without knowing you need to have money set aside for these additional fees.

LOAN ESTIMATE (LE)

You will receive several documents when purchasing a mortgage, with the two biggest being the loan estimate and the closing disclosure. The loan estimate is what you get when you first start working with your mortgage broker, while the closing disclosure is provided closer to your close date.

This is an example of what your loan estimate will look like. I will discuss the information contained on each page after the graphic.

Save this Loan Estimate to compare with your Closing Disclosure.

Loan Estimate

DATE ISSUED
APPLICANTS

PROPERTY

SALE PRICE

LOAN TERM	30 years
PURPOSE	Purchase
PRODUCT	Fixed
LOAN TYPE	☐ Conventional ☒ FHA ☐ VA ☐ _____
LOAN ID #	1222191064
RATE LOCK	☐ NO ☒ YES, until 4/11/2022 at 5:00 PM EDT

*Before closing, your interest rate, points, and lender credits can change unless you lock the interest rate. All other estimated closing costs expire on **3/24/2022** at 5:00 PM EDT*

Loan Terms

Loan Terms		Can this amount increase after closing?
Loan Amount	$427,121	**NO**
Interest Rate	4.375%	**NO**
Monthly Principal & Interest See Projected Payments below for your Estimated Total Monthly Payment	$2,132.56	**NO**
		Does the loan have these features?
Prepayment Penalty		**NO**
Balloon Payment		**NO**

Projected Payments

Payment Calculation	Years 1 - 30	
Principal & Interest		$2,132.56
Mortgage Insurance	+	295
Estimated Escrow Amount can increase over time	+	703
Estimated Total Monthly Payment		**$3,131**

Estimated Taxes, Insurance & Assessments Amount can increase over time	$703 a month	**This estimate includes** ☒ Property Taxes ☒ Homeowner's Insurance ☐ Other:	**In escrow?** YES YES	

See Section G on page 2 for escrowed property costs. You must pay for other property costs separately.

Costs at Closing

Estimated Closing Costs	$18,435	Includes $10,937 in Loan Costs + $7,498 in Other Costs -$0 in Lender Credits. See page 2 for details.
Estimated Cash to Close	$25,010	Includes Closing Costs See Calculating Cash to Close on page 2 for details.

Visit **www.consumerfinance.gov/mortgage-estimate** for general information and tools.

The first page of your loan estimate shows your loan terms at the top, which include how much your loan is for, the interest rate, and your monthly principal and interest costs. In the second section, you will see your projected monthly payment, with a breakdown of how much goes to your principal and interest, how much goes to mortgage insurance, and how much goes into your escrow account (which is what will pay for your taxes, insurance, and assessments, as discussed above). The last section tells you how much you will need for closing costs and the estimated amount of cash you need to close.

Those last two lines can be confusing, especially for first-time buyers. It does *not* mean that you need a total of $43,445 to close. This means that your closing costs are estimated at $18,435. When you add your down payment amount to the closing costs, that is the amount you need to close: in this case, $25,010.

SECOND PAGE

Closing Cost Details

Loan Costs	
A. Origination Charges	**$111**
0.026% of Loan Amount (Points)	$111

B. Services You Cannot Shop For	**$8,259**
Appraisal Fee	$800
Credit Report	$80
Electronic Registration (MERS) Fee	$25
Flood Certification	$8
Mortgage Insurance Premium	$7,346

C. Services You Can Shop For	**$2,567**
Title - Mobile Notary Fee (Travel-Not Notarize)	$200
Title - New Loan Service Fee	$430
Title - Premium for Lender's Coverage	$1,197
Title - Recording Fee	$15
Title - Settlement Or Closing Fee	$725

D. TOTAL LOAN COSTS (A + B + C)	**$10,937**

Other Costs		
E. Taxes and Other Government Fees		**$160**
Recording Fees and Other Taxes		$160
Transfer Taxes		
F. Prepaids		**$4,024**
Homeowner's Insurance Premium (12 months)		$3,000
Mortgage Insurance Premium (months)		
Prepaid Interest ($51.20 per day for 20 days @ 4.375%)		$1,024
Property Taxes (months)		

G. Initial Escrow Payment at Closing		**$2,563**
Homeowner's Insurance	$250.00 per month for 3 mo.	$750
Mortgage Insurance	per month for mo.	
Property Taxes	$453.13 per month for 4 mo.	$1,813

H. Other		**$751**
Title - Owner's Title Policy (Optional)		$751

I. TOTAL OTHER COSTS (E + F + G + H)		**$7,498**

J. TOTAL CLOSING COSTS		**$18,435**
D + I		$18,435
Lender Credits		

Calculating Cash to Close	
Total Closing Costs (J)	$18,435
Closing Costs Financed (Paid from your Loan Amount)	$0
Down Payment/Funds from Borrower	$7,879
Deposit	-$2,000
Funds for Borrower	$0
Seller Credits	$0
Adjustments and Other Credits	$696
Estimated Cash to Close	**$25,010**

Page 2

The second page details the specifics of your closing costs.

In Section A, you will see your origination charges. In this example, the buyer chose to buy down their interest rate for $111.

Section B shows all of the fees that come from your lender that you cannot shop around for, meaning you can't choose another company to do the appraisal on the home you want to buy or another company to run your credit report. In Section C, however, are the fees that you can shop around to get the best rate. These are all fees that relate to your title.

Section D is the total of Sections A, B, and C. However, this number won't be completely accurate because it includes your mortgage insurance, which is not an amount you need at closing. The mortgage insurance will only be paid as part of your monthly payment.

Section E shows your recording and transfer taxes. Section F is all of your prepaids that we discussed above. Prepaid interest is the interest you accrue before the day you close. For instance, if you are closing on the tenth of the month, you have twenty days of interest that are going to accrue before you make your first payment. That amount is what your prepaid interest line shows. This benefits you as the buyer because it gives you time before you have to make your first payment.

Section G shows the initial escrow payment, meaning how much money you need to put into your escrow so that there's enough to pay your taxes and insurance until your monthly payments start and money begins being added into the escrow account on a consistent basis.

Section H is the fee for the owner title policy, which while listed as optional, is very rarely optional. Section I is just the combination of totals of Sections E, F, G, and H, while Section J is the total of your loan costs (Section D) and other costs (Section I).

The last section shows you how much you need at closing. It takes your total closing costs from Section J and adds your down payment amount (pulled from the first page). It subtracts any earnest money deposit (EMD) you paid to make your contract valid when putting an offer on the house, because that EMD is just a credit toward these costs. If the seller is paying any of your closing costs, any funds are given to you, or there are any other credits you will receive, those reductions will show in this area as well. You are left with the estimated cash you need to close on the house.

You'll find that your numbers may be high on your loan estimate, but lower on your closing disclosure. That's because the government will not let lenders show discounts on your loan estimate. Your lender has to show the maximum amount your fees could cost. Then, in the closing disclosure, the fees can be reduced to what they really are.

When you get your loan estimate, have your lender walk you through what each line means.

Additional Information About This Loan

LENDER
NMLS/CA LICENSE ID
LOAN OFFICER
NMLS/CA LICENSE ID
EMAIL
PHONE

MORTGAGE BROKER
NMLS/CA LICENSE ID
LOAN OFFICER
NMLS/CA LICENSE ID
EMAIL
PHONE

Comparisons		Use these measures to compare this loan with other loans.
In 5 Years	$156,993	Total you will have paid in principal, interest, mortgage insurance, and loan costs.
	$38,510	Principal you will have paid off.
Annual Percentage Rate (APR)	5.397%	Your costs over the loan term expressed as a rate. This is not your interest rate.
Total Interest Percentage (TIP)	79.982%	The total amount of interest that you will pay over the loan term as a percentage of your loan amount.

Other Considerations

Appraisal	We may order an appraisal to determine the property's value and charge you for this appraisal. We will promptly give you a copy of any appraisal, even if your loan does not close. You can pay for an additional appraisal for your own use at your own cost.
Assumption	If you sell or transfer this property to another person, we ☒ will allow, under certain conditions, this person to assume this loan on the original terms. ☐ will not allow assumption of this loan on the original terms.
Homeowner's Insurance	This loan requires homeowner's insurance on the property, which you may obtain from a company of your choice that we find acceptable.
Late Payment	If your payment is more than *15* days late, we will charge a late fee of *4% of the overdue payment of Principal and Interest (P&I)*.
Refinance	Refinancing this loan will depend on your future financial situation, the property value, and market conditions. You may not be able to refinance this loan.
Servicing	We intend: ☒ to service your loan. If so, you will make your payments to us. ☐ to transfer servicing of your loan.

Confirm Receipt

By signing, you are only confirming that you have received this form. You do not have to accept this loan because you have signed or received this form.

_____
Date

The third page of your loan estimate compares your loan over five years. The first line tells you how much you will have paid in principal interest, mortgage insurance, and loan costs over the next five years. This amount is how much equity you have in your home, before you consider how much the home has increased in value. In other words, this is cash in your pocket, plus whatever your down payment was, should you sell your home at this point.

The second line is your annual percentage rate, which is *not* your interest rate. APR was originally created so you could shop around between different lenders to find the best rate. To figure out your APR, they calculate how your payment is in rate form. For example, if your loan was for $100,000 at 3 percent interest rate for thirty years, and your down payment was $10,000, your actual loan was for $90,000. Your APR will show, in percentage form, what a $90,000 loan with a 3 percent interest rate for thirty years is. This can be very confusing, and honestly, it's rarely used anymore.

Lastly is your total interest percentage, which is the total amount of interest that you will pay over the entire life of the loan, again shown as a percentage.

The important thing to know is that your loan estimate can only reduce in price. Housing laws state that your loan estimate is the max amount of charges that can occur. If there are any increases, your lender will have to either eat the costs, or cancel the loan and start all over. The purpose of your loan estimate is to show you the maximum amount your final numbers can be.

CLOSING DISCLOSURE (CD)

Once all of the fees are finalized, you will receive your closing disclosure, which tells you exactly what your final numbers are. There will most likely be a difference from your loan estimate, anywhere from $300 to $1,500 lower. The numbers you see on your closing disclosure are exactly what you are going to see on your loan documents.

Your closing disclosure shows you the same information as your loan estimate, just broken down in a format that you would see at escrow. Let's look at what the information means.

FIRST PAGE

Closing Disclosure

This form is a statement of final loan terms and closing costs. Compare this document with your Loan Estimate.

Closing Information	Transaction Information	Loan Information
Date Issued	**Borrower**	**Loan Term** 30 years
Closing Date		**Purpose** Purchase
Disbursement Date		**Product** Fixed
Settlement Agent		
File #	**Seller**	**Loan Type** ☐ Conventional ☒ FHA
Property		☐ VA ☐ _____
		Loan ID #
Sale Price		**MIC #**
	Lender	

Loan Terms

		Can this amount increase after closing?
Loan Amount	$427,121	**NO**
Interest Rate	4.375%	**NO**
Monthly Principal & Interest See Projected Payments below for your Estimated Total Monthly Payment	$2,132.56	**NO**
		Does the loan have these features?
Prepayment Penalty		**NO**
Balloon Payment		**NO**

Projected Payments

Payment Calculation	Years 1 - 30
Principal & Interest	$2,132.56
Mortgage Insurance	+ 295.11
Estimated Escrow *Amount can increase over time*	+ 611.21
Estimated Total Monthly Payment	**$3,038.88**

Estimated Taxes, Insurance & Assessments *Amount can increase over time* *See page 4 for details*	$611.21 a month	**This estimate includes** ☒ Property Taxes ☒ Homeowner's Insurance ☐ Other: *See Escrow Account on page 4 for details. You must pay for other property costs separately.*	**In escrow?** YES YES

Costs at Closing

Closing Costs	$18,158.68	Includes $10,937.06 in Loan Costs + $7,221.62 in Other Costs -$0 in Lender Credits. *See page 2 for details.*
Cash to Close	$24,733.58	Includes Closing Costs *See Calculating Cash to Close on page 3 for details.*

On the first page, you will see what your payment is, how much needs to be in your escrow, what your mortgage insurance amount will be, how much your closing costs will be, and how much cash you need to close.

Closing Cost Details

Loan Costs		Borrower-Paid		Seller-Paid		Paid by Others
		At Closing	Before Closing	At Closing	Before Closing	
A. Origination Charges		**$111.05**				
01 0.026% of Loan Amount (Points)		$111.05				
02 Origination Fee to Lending for Living, Inc						
03						
04						
05						
06						
07						
08						
B. Services Borrower Did Not Shop For		**$8,259.01**				
01 Appraisal Fee	to TBD	$800.00				
02 Credit Report	to Other	$80.00				
03 Electronic Registration (MERS) Fee		$24.95				
04 Flood Certification		$8.00				
05 Mortgage Insurance Premium	to	$7,346.06				
06						
07						
08						
09						
10						
C. Services Borrower Did Shop For		**$2,567.00**				
01 Title - Mobile Notary Fee (Travel - Not Notarize) to First American Title Company		$200.00				
02 Title - New Loan Service Fee		$430.00				
03 Title - Premium for Lender's Coverage		$1,197.00				
04 Title - Recording Fee		$15.00				
05 Title - Settlement Or Closing Fee		$725.00				
06						
07						
08						
D. TOTAL LOAN COSTS (Borrower-Paid)		**$10,937.06**				
Loan Costs Subtotals (A + B + C)		$10,937.06				

Other Costs						
E. Taxes and Other Government Fees		**$160.00**				
01 Recording Fees Deed: $36.00 Mortgage: $124.00		$160.00				
02						
F. Prepaids		**$4,023.92**				
01 Homeowner's Insurance Premium (12 mo.)		$3,000.00				
02 Mortgage Insurance Premium (mo.)						
03 Prepaid Interest ($51.20 per day from 4/11/22 to 5/1/22)		$1,023.92				
04 Property Taxes (mo.)						
05						
G. Initial Escrow Payment at Closing		**$2,286.70**				
01 Homeowner's Insurance $158.08 per month for 3 mo.		$474.24				
02 Mortgage Insurance per month for mo.						
03 Property Taxes $453.13 per month for 4 mo.		$1,812.52				
04						
05						
06						
07						
08 Aggregate Adjustment		-$0.06				
H. Other		**$751.00**				
01 Buyers Agent Real Estate Commission				$13,050.00		
02 Sellers Agent Real Estate Commission				$13,050.00		
03 Title - Owner's Title Policy (Optional)		$751.00				
04						
05						
06						
07						
08						
I. TOTAL OTHER COSTS (Borrower-Paid)		**$7,221.62**				
Other Costs Subtotals (E + F + G + H)		$7,221.62				
J. TOTAL CLOSING COSTS (Borrower-Paid)		**$18,158.68**				
Closing Costs Subtotals (D + I)		$18,158.68		$26,100.00		$8,542.42
Lender Credits						

Your second page shows your closing costs in more detail, and it should either match your loan estimate exactly or it can be a little less. However, while your loan estimate shows all of the information in two columns, your closing disclosure is shown in a single column, similar to what you will see when you close.

This page shows you what everyone is making during this transaction so you are fully aware of all the fees going on that are not on the loan estimate. You see everyone's information, including how much is being paid to the agents as commission.

THIRD PAGE

Calculating Cash to Close

Use this table to see what has changed from your Loan Estimate.

	Loan Estimate	Final	Did this change?
Total Closing Costs (J)	$18,435.00	$18,158.68	YES • See **Total Loan Costs(D)** and **Total Other Costs(I)**
Closing Costs Paid Before Closing	$0	$0	NO
Closing Costs Financed (Paid from your Loan Amount)	$0	$0	NO
Down Payment/Funds from Borrower	$7,879.00	$7,879.00	NO
Deposit	-$2,000.00	-$2,000.00	NO
Funds for Borrower	$0	$0	NO
Seller Credits	$0	$0	NO
Adjustments and Other Credits	$696.00	$695.90	YES • See details in **Sections K and L**
Cash to Close	$25,010.00	$24,733.58	

Summaries of Transactions

Use this table to see a summary of your transaction.

BORROWER'S TRANSACTION

K. Due from Borrower at Closing	$453,854.58
01 Sale Price of Property	$435,000.00
02 Sale Price of Any Personal Property Included In Sale	
03 Closing Costs Paid at Closing (J)	$18,158.68
04	
Adjustments	
05	
06	
07	
Adjustments for Items Paid by Seller in Advance	
08 City/Town Taxes 5/6/22 to 7/1/22	$695.90
09 County Taxes to	
10 Assessments to	
11	
12	
13	
14	
15	

L. Paid Already by or on Behalf of Borrower at Closing	$429,121.00
01 Deposit (EMD: $2,000.00 / Cash Deposit: $0.00)	$2,000.00
02 Loan Amount	$427,121.00
03 Existing Loan(s) Assumed or Taken Subject to	
04	
05 Seller Credit	$0.00
Other Credits	
06	
07	
Adjustments	
08	
09	
10	
11	
Adjustments for Items Unpaid by Seller	
12 City/Town Taxes to	
13 County Taxes to	
14 Assessments to	
15	
16	
17	

SELLER'S TRANSACTION

M. Due to Seller at Closing	$435,695.90
01 Sale Price of Property	$435,000.00
02 Sale Price of Any Personal Property Included In Sale	
03	
04	
05	
06	
07	
08	
Adjustments for Items Paid by Seller in Advance	
09 City/Town Taxes 5/6/22 to 7/1/22	$695.90
10 County Taxes to	
11 Assessments to	
12	
13	
14	
15	
16	

N. Due from Seller at Closing	$26,100.00
01 Excess Deposit	
02 Closing Costs Paid at Closing (J)	$26,100.00
03 Existing Loan(s) Assumed or Taken Subject to	
04 Payoff of First Mortgage Loan	
05 Payoff of Second Mortgage Loan	
06	
07	
08 Seller Credit	$0.00
09	
10	
11	
12	
13	
Adjustments for Items Unpaid by Seller	
14 City/Town Taxes to	
15 County Taxes to	
16 Assessments to	
17	
18	
19	

CALCULATION	
Total Due from Borrower at Closing (K)	$453,854.58
Total Paid Already by or on Behalf of Borrower at Closing (L)	-$429,121.00
Cash to Close ☒ From ☐ To Borrower	**$24,733.58**

CALCULATION	
Total Due to Seller at Closing (M)	$435,695.90
Total Due from Seller at Closing (N)	-$26,100.00
Cash to Close ☐ From ☒ To Seller	**$409,595.90**

Page 3

At the top of the third page, you will see a side-by-side comparison of your loan estimate and the closing disclosure. As you can see in this example, there was a difference of $300, which means the lender didn't put too many costs in the loan estimate.

As you move down the page, there is a summary of the transaction, with the buyer's side on the left and seller side on the right. Unlike the loan estimate, the closing disclosure has the sales price of the property.

At the bottom of the buyer's side, it shows how much is due from the buyer at closing, which is the sale price of the house plus the closing costs, how much is being paid by the loan, and how much is left for the buyer to pay with cash (i.e., your down payment and closing costs). On the seller side, it shows how much is due to the seller minus their closing costs.

FOURTH PAGE

Additional Information About This Loan

Loan Disclosures

Assumption
If you sell or transfer this property to another person, your lender
☒ will allow, under certain conditions, this person to assume this loan on the original terms.
☐ will not allow assumption of this loan on the original terms.

Demand Feature
Your loan
☐ has a demand feature, which permits your lender to require early repayment of the loan. You should review your note for details.
☒ does not have a demand feature.

Late Payment
If your payment is more than *15* days late, your lender will charge a late fee of *4% of the overdue payment of Principal and Interest (P&I)*.

Negative Amortization (Increase in Loan Amount)
Under your loan terms, you
☐ are scheduled to make monthly payments that do not pay all of the interest due that month. As a result, your loan amount will increase (negatively amortize), and your loan amount will likely become larger than your original loan amount. Increases in your loan amount lower the equity you have in this property.

☐ may have monthly payments that do not pay all of the interest due that month. If you do, your loan amount will increase (negatively amortize), and, as a result, your loan amount may become larger than your original loan amount. Increases in your loan amount lower the equity you have in this property.

☒ do not have a negative amortization feature.

Partial Payments
Your lender
☐ may accept payments that are less than the full amount due (partial payments) and apply them to your loan.
☐ may hold them in a separate account until you pay the rest of the payment, and then apply the full payment to your loan.
☒ does not accept any partial payments.
If this loan is sold, your new lender may have a different policy.

Security Interest
You are granting a security interest in

You may lose this property if you do not make your payments or satisfy other obligations for this loan.

Escrow Account
For now, your loan
☒ will have an escrow account (also called an "impound" or "trust" account) to pay the property costs listed below. Without an escrow account, you would pay them directly, possibly in one or two large payments a year. Your lender may be liable for penalties and interest for failing to make a payment.

Escrow		
Escrowed Property Costs over Year 1	$10,875.84	Estimated total amount over year 1 for your escrowed property costs: *Hazard Insurance Reserves* *Mortgage Insurance Reserve* *See attached page for additional information*
Non-Escrowed Property Costs over Year 1	$0.00	Estimated total amount over year 1 for your non-escrowed property costs: *Homeowners Association Dues* You may have other property costs.
Initial Escrow Payment	$2,286.70	A cushion for the escrow account you pay at closing. See Section G on page 2.
Monthly Escrow Payment	$906.32	The amount included in your total monthly payment.

☐ will not have an escrow account because ☐ you declined it ☐ your lender does not offer one. You must directly pay your property costs, such as taxes and homeowner's insurance. Contact your lender to ask if your loan can have an escrow account.

No Escrow	
Estimated Property Costs over Year 1	Estimated total amount over year 1. You must pay these costs directly, possibly in one or two large payments a year.
Escrow Waiver Fee	

In the future,
Your property costs may change and, as a result, your escrow payment may change. You may be able to cancel your escrow account, but if you do, you must pay your property costs directly. If you fail to pay your property taxes, your state or local government may (1) impose fines and penalties or (2) place a tax lien on this property. If you fail to pay any of your property costs, your lender may (1) add the amounts to your loan balance, (2) add an escrow account to your loan, or (3) require you to pay for property insurance that the lender buys on your behalf, which likely would cost more and provide fewer benefits than what you could buy on your own.

This page includes all of the specifics about your loan. The first section tells you what it will allow under certain conditions. For instance, in a market where interest rates are 8 percent, if someone wants to buy your house, they can assume your original loan and then get a loan for the difference.

The demand feature permits a lender to require early repayment of your loan. You never want your loan to have the demand feature checked. Without the demand feature, the only way your lender can make your loan due is if you transfer it to someone else's name without paying it off.

Negative amortization is when your monthly payment does not cover all the interest on your loan payment and that interest gets added onto your principal. This was common with the loans people had in 2002–2006, often referred to as neg-am loans. With neg-am loans, you could pick your payment: full payment, interest only, or no interest. If you chose no interest, the interest each month was added to the loan, which would lower the equity in the home.

Partial payments means if your payment is $1,500 and your loan allows partial payments, you could send in $750 instead. However, most loans require full payments.

The escrow account section, sometimes known as an impound or trust account, tells you how much you are putting in your escrow account and estimated costs over one year for the costs listed. Initial escrow payment is the amount you put in at closing as a cushion for your account, and your monthly escrow amount is your mortgage insurance, home insurance, and taxes that are added in every month to ensure that you don't get behind in your taxes or insurance, which could cost you your house.

Your mortgage broker will send you your closing disclosure a minimum of three days before closing, so you have time to look over all the information. Once you sign your closing disclosure, you have to wait three business days to sign your loan documents. In the past, you could sign it and then immediately sign your loan documents, which didn't give buyers a chance to understand what they were signing or make an informed purchase. Waiting three days makes for smarter consumers, and makes you less likely to be taken advantage of.

However, before you can get a loan estimate or closing disclosure, you have to know if you are pre-approved.

CHAPTER SIX

Shopping for Homes

Steve finally found the house of his dreams. He called up his real estate agent and said, "Hey Lisa. I found this amazing house for $400,000. Can we go see it?"

"Absolutely. How's 4 p.m. today?"

"Great." Steve meets Lisa at 4 p.m., and they take a tour. He knew this was the perfect house for him.

"I want to buy this house. Let's put an offer in."

"That's great news! Let's get you a prequalification letter to include with the purchase contract."

"A what?"

"A prequal letter. It's a letter from your mortgage broker that says you qualify for a mortgage to buy the home. It's easy to get. You just tell the mortgage broker how much you make, how much money you have in the bank, and they do a quick credit check."

"That sounds easy. Let's do it."

Lisa puts him in touch with a mortgage broker she knows and Steve gets prequalified for the home. Unfortunately, over 50 percent of the time, buyers who get prequalified for a home don't actually qualify. Steve found out that he was part of that 50 percent because when he went into underwriting, he was told he didn't qualify for a $400,000 mortgage.

A few days later, Lisa gets a call from a woman named Julie, who wants to see the same house. Julie tells her that she's already been pre-approved for the house by her mortgage broker, which meant that her mortgage broker knew she had the right amount of money for the down payment, her income was high enough, and her credit check was clear.

Julie falls in love with the house and puts in an offer with her pre-approval letter. The offer was accepted, underwriting went through without a hitch because she was already pre-approved, and she closed on the house a month later.

Both Steve and Julie were living in a pre-COVID world. Today, the process is not so simple. Thanks to cleaning restrictions and safety, you have to have a pre-approval letter before you can step foot in a home to view it.

Today, if Steve wanted to go see the house, the first question Lisa would ask him is, "Do you have your pre-approval letter?"

"My what?"

After Lisa explains what a pre-approval letter is and puts Steve in contact with a mortgage broker, he begins the process of getting his letter. Once he has it, Steve gives it to Lisa, who lets the seller know that Steve is pre-approved, and they can now go see the house.

Julie also contacts Lisa and tells her she wants to see the house. "Do you have your pre-approval letter?"

"I have a fully underwritten pre-approval."

Lisa is ecstatic. A fully underwritten pre-approval means that not only are you pre-approved, but your loan has gone through the Fannie Mae or Freddie Mac underwriting engine already, so the mortgage broker already knows that your loan can be finalized with no issues. When Julie puts an offer in on the house, it's accepted because Julie's letter told the seller she has everything needed to buy the house and that the process will progress faster, as it's already almost done.

Today, you need a fully underwritten pre-approval letter before you begin seeing homes, so you know what you can afford and so the selling agent and seller know that you can afford the home. Fully underwritten pre-approval is now the gold standard when purchasing homes. In a difficult buying market, it gives you a leg up and makes you more likely to be accepted.

PRE-QUALIFICATION

Pre-qualification is when a client tells their mortgage broker how much money they make and how much money they have in their bank account. Then, the lender runs their credit to verify how much debt they have, including their car payment, credit card debt, student loans, etc.

The problem with pre-qualification is that the client is telling the mortgage broker their income and assets, with no verification methods used. The mortgage broker is using their word to verify if they qualify for the house they want.

However, it's a common sentiment in the mortgage industry that pre-quals aren't worth the paper they're printed on. The reason is that most people don't understand how much they make, as we discussed in Chapter 2.

PRE-APPROVALS

For a pre-approval, your lender will verify your income and assets using the last two years of W-2s, thirty days of pay stubs, and two months of bank statements. Often, we find that you make more income than you think, because you are looking at your net income, not your gross income.

(As a reminder, your gross income is the full amount of money you make before taxes, while net is what you get in your paycheck.)

Pre-approvals also look at your credit, and your mortgage broker will confirm your liabilities and debts. Because they have an accurate income number, they can also calculate an accurate debt-to-income ratio as well.

With all of this information obtained and verified, your mortgage broker can more accurately let you know how much home you can afford. This number is the most you can afford and is essentially set in stone, unless your income or other information changes.

At my firm, and many others, we will only perform pre-approvals and fully underwritten pre-approvals because we don't want to risk our clients being unable to qualify for and close on the home they love. It results in a lot fewer cancellations of contracts for the mortgage broker and the buyer, and it benefits the seller because if the transaction doesn't go through the first time, the second offer is generally for a lower amount of money than the first.

It saves time, money, and heartache. Losing the house you love because you didn't qualify correctly is like failing an important test. It's like reliving your first big heartbreak.

FULLY UNDERWRITTEN PRE-APPROVED

This is the best option for all homebuyers. The only time I don't do a fully underwritten pre-approval is if my client urgently needs a letter on the weekend and the underwriter can't work.

By getting fully underwritten pre-approved, the only reason you won't get the house is if there's something wrong with it and you want to back out.

For this type of letter, your mortgage broker will follow all of the steps for pre-approval letters. Then, we take your information and put it through the Fannie Mae or Freddie Mac underwriting engines to verify that you qualify for the loan program you picked.

These underwriting system engines use algorithms to figure out whether or not the numbers you put to it will qualify that buyer for that home. The reason we use automated underwriting is because even if we know for a fact that your debt-to-income ratio is within the limits and your credit score is high enough, the engine may kick out your loan and say you don't qualify because of something we don't know about. These engines are standard in the industry, and every mortgage broker uses the same ones.

While pre-approval letters can be enough, sometimes there's a small reason you won't get approved, such as your credit score or a slightly too high debt-to-income ratio or some reason we are unsure of. By getting underwritten ahead of time, you can ensure 100 percent that your loan is going to be approved with no issues.

If your loan gets kicked out, your next steps depend on the reason your loan was denied. If your credit is too low, we can put together a plan to increase it. If there's something on your credit report, then we can work to get it removed. Whatever the reason, your lender will help you fix it, but you have to go through the process first.

PRE-QUAL VS. PRE-APPROVED VS. FULLY UNDERWRITTEN

The easiest way to explain the difference between these three types is with an analogy.

Martha is trying to get a new job that requires a college degree. When she does her pre-interview talk with the recruiter, Martha tells them that yes, she definitely has a college degree, and the recruiter moves her on to the next stage in the process.

This is the same as a pre-qual letter: the recruiter is relying on nothing but Martha's word at this point, just as a mortgage broker is relying on a buyer's word about their income and assets.

Martha arrives for her in-person interview, and she brings with her a copy of her degree from the university that she went to. The interviewer is impressed.

This is her pre-approval letter: she is proving her credentials to the interviewer, just like a buyer is proving their income and assets to the mortgage broker.

Once the interview is over, the company reaches out to the university to confirm that Martha went there and graduated. The university confirms her degree, and Martha gets hired.

This is the fully underwritten pre-approval: the company is verifying that everything is correct, just like the mortgage broker will ensure that your loan is approved.

NEVER CHOOSE PRE-QUALIFICATION

I said it above, and I am saying it again: never settle for pre-qualification. Too many times your loan will fall out.

Say you told your mortgage broker that you make $17 an hour and work 40 hours a week. But, once they see your pay stubs, they find that while sometimes you work forty hours a week, you often work less than that. Once you average your hours, it turns out you only average 33 hours a week. At this point, your mortgage broker has to average your income. Those seven hours could be enough to disqualify you from getting the loan amount.

You should always get at least a pre-approval, but if possible, get fully underwritten pre-approval. It protects you and it looks the best to the seller, increasing the odds that your contract will be accepted.

JEREMIAH AND THE MISSING LOAN

Jeremiah was a client who wanted to buy the home he was currently leasing. When I was qualifying him, he showed no issues. However, when you get an FHA or VA loan, we have to put your information through a program called CAIVRS, which verifies that you have no federal debt and you are not delinquent on your student loans.

When I put in Jeremiah's information, he showed a student loan on CAIVRS that had gone bad, meaning that he had not paid on one of his student loans. This loan was from one of the colleges that was in the news several years ago for giving student loans to anyone who asked for one. After he graduated, he called to try and make a payment on it, but they told him he didn't owe anything. A few months later, he received a letter saying he did owe on it.

Then COVID happened, and no one was reporting student loan debts while the economy was struggling. Finally, COVID restrictions loosened and student loan debt companies started reporting again. So, even though he had tried to pay, he was reported as being delinquent, and the loan was flagged on CAIVRS.

Once we found out he was flagged in CAIVRS, he was able to contact the student loan company that had reported him. They reconciled it, meaning they made the loan current instead of delinquent. Now that it was current, he was able to pay on it. It took three payments before the loan could be removed from the CAIVRS system. Once it was removed five months later (one month to get the loan current, three months of payments, and one month to have it removed from CAIVRS), we could restart the entire loan process, where his loan was approved and he could finally close on the house.

Jeremiah's story is a great example of unforeseen issues that can come up if you don't get a fully underwritten pre-approval. There may be something you don't know about until your information gets run, and you don't want to lose the house of your dreams because you didn't know of any issues ahead of time. Avoid heartbreak by getting your loan approved before you put in a contract.

LISTING AGENTS AND SELLERS CARE TOO

Both listing agents and owners will look at what type of approval letter you have, with the listing agent explaining which offers are best to the owner.

Say an owner gets four offers on their home. Their listing agent is going to put them in order from worst to best offer: pre-qual, pre-approval, fully underwritten pre-approval, and cash. However, cash doesn't always win out over the other three because it isn't always at the right price. If the cash offer isn't right, they will look at the fully underwritten pre-approvals because they know that that loan will close as it's already been fully underwritten. If that offer isn't right, they will look at the pre-approval offer, as it's most likely to go through, and finally at the pre-qual, though they won't recommend those as they only have a 50 percent chance to close.

Adam is selling his home and gets four offers, all for $450,000. Joe sends in a pre-qual offer, Julie's is pre-approved, Mark's is fully underwritten, and David's is cash. Lisa, Adam's listing agent, sits down with him to go over the four offers.

"Joe's offer is a pre-qual offer, so you don't want to pick this one. Because of how a pre-qual offer is made, we don't actually know if he can qualify for this house."

"Great, who is next?"

"Next we have Julie. She has a great offer, but Mark's is better because while Julie's is most likely to actually get her mortgage approved, Mark is definitely going to get approved. He's a sure bet."

"Okay, what about David?"

"David's offer is cash, so it's going to be the best offer for you. No waiting for a mortgage to get approved! We can close whenever you both want."

Now let's go through some other scenarios with this group of offers.

Say Julie has 25 percent for the down payment and so does Joe. Julie is going to be a great offer because if the appraisal comes in low, they know she has enough money to make up the difference using the extra cash in her down payment. Joe is still not a great option, because there's no guarantee his offer will go through.

Down payment amount is just one of the factors that owners and listing agents will review. Others include what loan program you are using: FHA, VA, or conventional. Most of the time, owners will choose cash, then conventional, then VA, then FHA. The reason is because of the false idea that conventional appraisal guidelines are the most lax, while VA and FHA appraisals are more strict. In reality, they are all about the same.

Another factor is when the person wants to close on the house. If the cash offer doesn't want to close for a month, but the pre-approval offer can close right away, they may pick the pre-approval offer.

They also look at if the person is buying the house for a rental. If the sellers like their neighbors, they may not want to sell it to someone who won't even be living there. Seller circumstances can dictate which offer is chosen. If the seller is a Veteran, they may choose the VA loan offer because they want to help another Vet.

Some advice if you have a VA loan is to have your mortgage broker contact the listing agent and explain your situation. Often listing agents don't know that today's VA loan program is very different from the old version. The old version used to have non-allowables and other items that made it harder to get your offer accepted, but today those have been removed. Unfortunately, a lot of agents are unaware of these changes. It also helps if your mortgage broker can tell them that you have money in the bank and that you're not using it simply because the VA loan doesn't require a down payment. Knowing you have cash if the appraisal is low can make a big difference in whether or not your offer gets chosen.

A last factor that can be considered is if you are waiving contingencies on your inspection. This means that you will still get an inspection, but that the seller is not required to fix any issues that show. You are buying the house as-is, which can be ideal for a seller who doesn't want to pay for any unknown issues before they are out of the house. Under law, however, the seller does have to disclose if they are aware of any issues the house has.

You can also waive the appraisal contingency. An appraisal is when a professional comes out and verifies that the house is worth what you are paying for it. If the sale contract is for $400,000, the appraiser is going to ensure that the house is worth $400,000. If they say the house is only worth $380,000 and you've waived the appraisal contingency, you have to pay the $20,000 difference from your bank account, with gift money, or with some other asset.

In today's market, if you want to buy a home, make sure you are getting a fully underwritten pre-approval, as that will guarantee 99.9 percent of the time that your loan is going to close and you'll get the house you want. When you work with the right mortgage broker, buying a house should be such an easy process that you want to do it again. It shouldn't be like you are living in a horror movie.

Once you have your fully underwritten pre-approval and you

find the house you want, it's time to get into the contract process.

CHAPTER SEVEN

The Contract Process

A close friend of mine, Matt, unknowingly made a costly mistake when he recently tried to buy a duplex in a small village in the Tahoe area of Nevada. Unfortunately, I couldn't help him as it was in an area where I am not registered to provide loans, so he had to use a different company.

When he put in his contract, he included an appraisal contingency, loan contingency, and inspection contingency (all three will be discussed in detail later in this chapter)—something of a novelty in that area, where sellers are reluctant to agree to any contingencies at all. Most homes in Southern California and in Nevada have their contingencies released the moment your contract is accepted, meaning that your earnest money deposit (EMD)—usually 1 percent of the home's purchase price—is no longer yours.

This sounds like the ideal situation, but I received a call from Matt a few weeks into the contract. He was extremely distraught. "I need your help," he said. "I need to see if I can get my earnest money deposit back because I'm not going to be able to get a loan on this property now."

I went through his contract and found that although he had those three contingencies, he had released them, essentially voiding their protection, the week before because he had no choice. He had been given a Notice to Perform by the seller, meaning that he had three days to release those contingencies or else the seller was going to cancel the contract.

Matt didn't want to lose the property, so he released all three contingencies, even the loan contingency, which would have protected him if his loan didn't go through. As soon as he released those contingencies, his EMD of $25,000 was now technically the seller's money. Releasing contingencies tells the seller that you are going to close, and if you don't, they get to keep the deposit.

Matt didn't understand why he wasn't receiving his EMD. Often, real estate agents don't explain details such as contingencies very well to their clients, so they don't always know the down-side of what they are doing. Matt's agent didn't explain that by releasing the contingencies, he was losing the protection of his EMD if his loan wasn't finalized. Instead, his agent told Matt, "You have to release the contingencies, or else you're going to lose the house."

After the contingencies were released, Matt found out that he would have to provide specific documentation to the mortgage broker that he was unable to provide. No documents meant a denied loan, and because he released the contingencies, that meant he was out $25,000.

While I couldn't help him with his loan, I put him into contact with another mortgage broker who may have been able to help. Unfortunately, he was already three weeks into a four-week contract. With only one week left in the process, the new mortgage broker wasn't able to finalize and get approval in time for the closing, and the seller had a backup cash offer on the property, so he had no incentive to push the closing back. After all, he was going to potentially get $25,000 from Matt and cash from the backup offer.

Because Matt didn't have all of the information about what releasing those contingencies meant for him, and because he didn't have the right lender to begin with, he lost his $25,000 and the property.

If he had been fully aware that he could have lost that money, he could have made an informed decision on whether or not to risk his money or let the property go and find another one. He also would have known to talk to his loan officer before releasing the loan contingency, which could have protected him.

It's essential that you know the process of getting into a contract and know that a contract is a legally binding agreement. Once it is signed, you are bound to the terms, which can include losing huge sums of money.

WHAT IS A CONTRACT?

When you see the word contract used in reference to purchasing a home, it is referring to the offer you, the buyer, send to the seller to purchase a home. While a contract's appearance may look different from state to state, they all have one thing in common: they are a true contract. This means, when you write the contract (or, more realistically, when your real estate agent writes your contract), in order for it to be valid, you have to include an EMD.

Let's look at an example. Mark wants to purchase a house for $450,000. He's putting 20 percent down—$90,000—and he needs to include an EMD, which is usually 1 percent of the purchase price. Mark's agent has him wire the $4,500 EMD to escrow when his offer is accepted.

Mark's contract includes:

- The buyer's full name (Mark Wellborn)
- Address of the property he wants to purchase
- Name of the listing agent and their firm
- Name of the buying agent and their firm
- Terms of the purchase
  - The amount he's willing to pay for the house ($450,000)
  - His down payment amount minus EMD ($85,500)
  - How much his loan is for ($360,000)
  - What type of qualification he has (fully underwritten pre-approval)
- How long until close of escrow (30 days, 15 days, or a specific date)
- How many days this contract is good for (twenty-four hours, three days, etc.)
- How much his EMD is ($4,500)
- Any additional finance terms (how long he has after the seller accepts the offer to verify his down payment and money for closing costs, etc.)
- How long until loan contingencies need to be removed

Contingencies are ways that the buyer can get out of the contract if they need or want to. The most popular ones are loan contingency, appraisal contingency, and investigation of property contingency. Once you release these contingencies, usually within seventeen to twenty-one days, your EMD is on the line. This means if you back out of the contract after you release your contingencies, you lose your EMD, i.e., the seller gets to keep that money.

On your contract, you can specify which contingencies you want to have or not have, and how long you have to release them after the contract is signed.

Say you have an appraisal contingency with a seventeen-day period, and the appraisal comes in at the correct amount within fifteen days. The buyer releases that contingency because they no longer need it.

Your contract also has obligations that come with it. On your contract, you are going to list possession, which means when you are going to get the house. That can be as soon as it closes, five o'clock on the day it records, or maybe the seller can't move into their new place yet, so you can include that they are renting it back from you for a certain amount of time.

If you choose the day it records, that means that the loan funds are sent to escrow, escrow pays everything off and sends the grant deed (the paper that says the seller has granted you the property) to the county recorder's office because everything in the transaction has gone through as it should. Once the county recorder's office has proof (i.e., the grant deed), that property is now legally your home.

Obligations also include what items in the house are included or excluded, such as refrigerators, dishwashers, ovens, etc. It's important to ensure that if you want an appliance or item that is already in the house, you list it in your contract or the seller is not obligated to leave it for you. For instance, if you want the standalone bookshelves that the seller has in the study, you need to list them on your contract. Anything fixed to the house is usually considered part of the house in terms of the sale.

When you send your contract to the seller, they can counter your offer, which means that they don't like one or more of the terms you've included. They may want to change something, remove something, or add something.

They send you back a new contract, which is called the counteroffer. If you accept their counteroffer, you sign the new contract and are now in escrow. This is considered a true contract because you've signed a legal document and given your EMD. The contract is now valid.

Once a contract is valid, you have to fulfill all of the terms and conditions. For instance, if you don't release a contingency by the agreed-upon date, the seller agent and seller will send you what's called a Notice to Perform. If you don't perform (in this case, release the contingency), they can cancel your escrow. Your EMD will still be yours in this particular case because you didn't release the contingency, but your contract is now void, meaning the seller can now sell to someone else.

When it comes to offers and counteroffers, you don't get just one shot. The buyer and seller can send offers back and forth as many times as you want until you agree. I've had clients go through seven counteroffers before they were in agreement.

Purchase contracts can be sixteen pages or more. They break down who is paying for what fee, such as whether the seller is paying for the escrow fees or if you are splitting the fees 50/50. Your agent will walk you through every option, and explain to you what each item means. This is why it's so important to have a good agent because if they check the wrong box, it could cost you money.

HAVING THE RIGHT AGENT IS EVERYTHING

Having the right agent is like having the right doctor or the right lawyer. They should be a professional who is working full-time for you. They should know your needs and wants, support you, and make sure you don't have any issues when you are buying the property.

Your agent is helping you with the largest purchase you will ever buy in your life. The agent should understand the importance of that responsibility.

I always suggest that you get a referral from someone you know and trust to help find your agent. Once you have a name, verify who they are, check their reviews, and if possible, check with any other clients they've had whom you may know.

Ask your friends, family, coworkers, boss, or community group, such as a church, who they've used in the past. If you don't have someone to ask, you can talk to your mortgage broker who helped you get pre-approved. Most mortgage brokers have agents that they work with and trust.

When my clients ask me for a recommendation, I try to play matchmaker. I have several agents that I work with, so I have a great recommendation for every one of my clients. For instance, I have one agent who has an advanced degree and is older: I send my older clients to him. For my younger clients, I send them to one of my younger agent partners. My Veteran clients I send to an agent who is also a Veteran and knows how today's VA loans work extremely well.

I also make sure to match my clients and agents based on personality. If a client needs hand-holding, I won't match them with an agent who is very direct and may come across as harsh. I want my clients to have the same excellent experience with their agent that they have with me.

AGENT RED FLAGS

A big red flag is if your agent doesn't return your calls or texts until the evening. This means they might not be a full-time agent—they most likely have another job during the day and only do real estate at night and on weekends. You want to work with an agent that does the job full-time. It's hard enough to stay on top of changes in the market when you are working 24/7—anything less and they'll miss valuable opportunities.

Another flag is if you don't feel like you are a priority to them. It's the same feeling you get when you're dating. If you aren't happy with the relationship, then reach back out to your network and find another agent to work with. You are not obligated to use the first agent you find.

Make sure that the agent is local to your area. Local people know the area best: they know the best neighborhoods and know where you want to live. You don't want someone from Sacramento selling you a house in San Diego. (This applies to your lender as well—someone from San Diego won't know the best loans for Tahoe.)

Say you see a listing for the house of your dreams, but you don't like your agent—one of those red flags is flying high. What do you do? Call the listing agent. The listing agent will be able to show you the house and then refer you to someone else on their team or in their firm. This way you don't lose out on the house, and you can try out another agent at the same time.

Check that your agent is a realtor, meaning that they have paid to be a part of the National Association of Realtors. This organization holds their members to a higher standard, which is great for their clients.

Other red flags include:

- Inexperience
- Poor communication
- Lack of professionalism (shows up late or no-shows)
- Encourages dishonesty
- Rude or pushy

The right agent will make you feel safe and confident when finding the perfect house for your needs.

GETTING INTO CONTRACT CAN TAKE TIME

Don't worry if your first offer doesn't get accepted. Today, getting into a contract can take several tries.

My clients George and Betty sold their house with a contingency stating that they were able to find another house before they closed. I referred them to one of my agent partners that they loved.

The agent showed the couple thirty-five houses. Of those thirty-five houses, they wrote offers for twenty of them. Finally, their twentieth offer was accepted—over two months after they started looking. This is for a couple who had 20 percent to put down. (Their buyer had to wait until George and Betty bought a new house before they could move in, thanks to the contingency George and Betty put in the contract.)

I know first-time homebuyers who have written twenty-five to thirty contracts before they got accepted. I advise you not to get discouraged if your first few offers don't go anywhere. Even when there is a more balanced market (versus a seller's market), it's not a guarantee that your first offer will get accepted.

When looking to buy a cabin, my wife and I thought we found the perfect property that was everything we wanted. We wrote an offer, but we ended up being a backup offer that was not needed. We looked at another cabin in the same neighborhood and wrote an offer on it—and it's the cabin we have now. Once we closed and moved in, we realized how glad we were that this was the cabin we bought.

I've found that the house you ultimately buy is the one that you are supposed to get. I've never talked to someone who said,

"Oh yeah, we just got this house. It's fine." They say, "We're so happy we got *this* house. We shopped forever, and this is the one we were meant to have."

Don't get distressed, and don't get discouraged. You have to be determined. It's the same as in business: 90 percent of people quit right before they're successful.

DON'T PAY FOR AN AGENT

In a transaction, there is a listing agent and a buyer agent. The seller of the house pays the listing agent and the buyer's agent. The listing contract will state how much they are paying each agent. This means that you, as a buyer, have no costs to the agents. However, that could always change.

You also don't have to use an agent to buy a home—unless the house is listed on the market. If you're buying from a family member or someone you know well, all you need to do is write your agreement on a piece of paper, and both parties sign it: "I agree to buy your house for $450,000. We will close in thirty days. We are paying normal escrow and title fees." (That last part means that each county has basic fees for closing costs for escrow and title, and usually the seller pays 50 percent of those fees and the buyer pays 50 percent of those fees.)

As long as both parties agree and sign, you can give that basic agreement to an escrow company and close without using any agents. However, if you want to make an offer on a house that's listed, you will want to have your own agent.

Nine times out of ten, you do not want to use the seller's agent, even if dual agency is allowed in your area (meaning that the listing agent and buyer agent are the same person). It's the same reason you don't want an attorney working on both sides of a case: how can you get the best deal for your seller and the best deal for your buyer at the same time? You want your own agent who is going to look out for your best interests only.

DON'T USE ALL THE APPS

Be very careful what homebuying apps you download on your phone and what you give them access to. There are some apps that, when you give them permission to do one thing, they actually get permission to do everything on your phone.

I had an agent friend who downloaded a popular app on his phone to do something for a client, and he accepted the standard rights. A few minutes later, someone from his church called him to ask him to list her house. Right after they hung up, she got a call from a stranger who had spoofed his number and said, "You don't want to work with Bob. You want to work directly with us."

When my friend researched the app, he found it had access to his pictures, email, voicemail, everything. The moral of the story is to be careful with what apps you download because they may be stealing your information.

If you want to look up homes yourself, I recommend realtor. com for most people. It uses the same MLS (multiple listing service) that agents use, so you will have access to all the best information. Of course, the best way to get information is through your agent, who will have the resources to obtain information that you can't find online.

Once you find your dream home and your contract is accepted, you can begin the loan process.

CHAPTER EIGHT

The Loan Process

Ben was fifty years old, self-employed, and trying to purchase a single-family home in Ripon, California. He first tried to get a loan through his bank. His bank had his paperwork for sixty days before finally telling him that they couldn't approve him. At this point, he was in contract on a property and frustrated—he wanted to close on this home. His real estate agent had told him from the beginning to work with my firm, but he wanted to stay loyal to his bank because they were the ones that handled his personal and business accounts.

Unfortunately, this is a common misconception. Unlike *It's A Wonderful Life*, your bank doesn't really care much about you. Just because you give them your money does not mean they'll bend over backward for you. It takes more than a handshake to get a house.

When Ben came to me, he was about to lose the house he wanted to buy, but I was able to help him quickly. Ben had a thirty-day contract on the property, and he had first approached the bank thirty days before the contract started. By the time he came to me, he had fifteen days left before the contract would end.

Ben didn't need a specialty loan. I was able to qualify him using a conventional loan putting 20 percent down. And because he was putting 20 percent down, I was able to get an appraisal waiver for his loan, meaning that he didn't need to get an appraisal on the property, allowing us to move through the process faster. The problem he was facing with the bank was that his company was an "off-year" company, meaning that his books don't run January to December but July to June. The bank didn't understand how his income worked in order to put it together for the loan documents. I did understand, and was able to put the paperwork together properly.

The total time it took for me to help him close, from the moment he came to me to the day he signed his final loan papers, was nine days. That's a huge difference from waiting two months to find out you can't get approved. Because I understood how his income and business worked, I was able to make the process easy and simple. All he needed to provide me was documentation on his income, his credit score, and money for the down payment. There was no reason to make the process any more difficult than that.

Ben was shocked at how fast I was able to get him the loan, when his bank was unable to do it after two months. He couldn't believe it at first, but he was ecstatic that he was going to get the house that he loved. (After he closed on the house, he switched banks.)

After the downturn, banks lost many of their good mortgage

people. This means that many banks don't have workers with decades of knowledge on how to get clients the right loan for them. Most of those workers are now employed at mortgage brokers. The people working at mortgage brokers have to get hours of education and relicensed every single year, ensuring they know what they are talking about and are up to date on all of the current changes to process and law.

When you work with a knowledgeable mortgage broker, they have already done most of the underwriter's job for them, because they know exactly what is needed. This is why it's so important for you to work with someone who understands every aspect of the loan process and can make it easy for you every step of the way.

THE LOAN PROCESS

The loan process starts the moment you get into contract, meaning that the moment the seller accepts and signs your contract offer, the loan period process begins. Your realtor will open escrow and let your mortgage broker know the name of the escrow company and all pertinent information.

Then, your mortgage broker, whom you should have been at least pre-approved by, will contact the escrow company to get their fees as these are part of your closing costs. The escrow company will also let the mortgage broker know who is paying for what (the seller versus the buyer).

Next, your mortgage broker will verify what time periods have been allotted for different aspects of the contract, because while there are standard time frames, sometimes the buyer or seller wants a longer or shorter time. While these time periods are handled by your Realtor—meaning they are the person who will formally release the contingencies built into your contract—it's important for your lender to know them as well because they are responsible for ordering some of the documentation, such as the appraisal (more on that in a minute).

Then, we start looking into your loan and how it works with your contract. Is there anything that needs updating, such as bank statements, pay stubs, or a credit check? Depending on how long you've been shopping for a home, you may need to have your credit checked again (your credit is usually good for 120 days). Getting your file in order quickly is essential, because as soon as your contract is signed by the seller, all contingency periods begin.

Of the three contingencies you can have on your contract (inspection, appraisal, and loan), the appraisal period is the most important. Remember, the appraisal is when a professional determines the current market value of the property. While every state (and sometimes every county in that state) has a standard time period for the appraisal, often that time period could be shortened by the seller from seventeen days to as low as seven days. In order for your lender to order the appraisal, they need to have received the fees they asked for from the escrow company and they need to put together the loan estimate.

The appraisal and the appraisal time period are important for a few reasons. One, depending on the type of loan you are using, the loan value cannot exceed the appraisal amount. Two, if you don't get an appraisal within the contract's stated time period, the seller could make you release the appraisal contingency. If that happens, you could either not get your loan at all (again, depending on the loan type) or you may have to purchase the house without knowing the true value of the house, resulting in you vastly overpaying for the property.

Your mortgage broker is responsible for ordering the appraisal and making sure it's completed within the allotted time period—however, they cannot order it until the loan estimate disclosure (discussed in detail in Chapter 5) is signed by all parties. Signing the loan estimate disclosure is acknowledgment from the buyer that the mortgage broker can start the loan process. Remember, the loan estimate disclosure will show the maximum amount for each closing fee. The final numbers may be smaller when you do close, but they will never be larger.

While most appraisals come back to the mortgage broker within seven to ten days, there are circumstances when the contingency period has been shortened or the appraisal companies are busy, and they can't return an amount within that time frame. In that case, you may have to pay a rush fee, which can typically range from $150–$250, though it can be more depending on the area and how quickly you need the appraisal turned around.

Once your mortgage broker orders the appraisal, they begin to gather all of the documents for the loan that you have already submitted, and order any extra documents that are now needed, such as employment verification. After the documents are gathered, we submit the loan to underwriting. The underwriter will relook at all of the documents and your loan contract, ensure everything looks good, and sign off on the loan, which means it now has conditional approval.

When you are conditionally approved, it means that there is still something the underwriter needs to provide full approval. Usually, the missing item is the final appraisal as the underwriter is working toward conditional approval at the same time as the appraisal is being ordered and completed. As part of the conditional approval, the underwriter will say that the loan needs an appraisal to come in at or under a specific dollar amount for full approval to be given. If your appraised value comes in higher, the home will sell for the original sale price. If your appraisal comes in lower, then you renegotiate with the seller.

There can be other conditions, however. For instance, the bank statement you provided may not be clear enough for the underwriter, so a new one needs to be sent. They may need four weeks of pay stubs, instead of the three weeks you provided because you were off one week. They could be waiting for the EMD to be showing in the escrow account, meaning the underwriter needs proof that escrow has received enough money for the down payment and closing costs. If you are getting gift money, you will need to provide the gift letter and have the money wired into escrow.

If you have had multiple jobs over the last two years, you may have missed sending one of the W-2s, so now the underwriter needs a verification of employment, which is a document your employer fills out stating how much you made last year and how much you made this year. Another condition could be that you need to provide a homeowner's insurance declaration page. When you get into the loan process, you may not know right away who your insurance company is going to be for the property, but proof of insurance is needed before the loan can close. The underwriter also needs to get the final wiring instructions from the escrow company and mortgage brokers, as well as the closing protection letter from the escrow company.

These are just a few of the examples of small, simple conditions that are easy to provide. Sometimes buyers get lucky and there are no conditions except the appraisal, proof of home insurance, and verification of EMD, because everything else was provided up front (this is more common when you've been fully underwritten pre-approved).

Today, underwriting usually takes one to three hours (during business hours), meaning you know if your loan is approved or denied within three hours.

If your loan comes back with conditional approval, your lender begins the process of getting those items from either you, the borrower, or from the escrow company. Typically escrow companies will provide documents or verification within twenty-four to forty-eight hours. You should provide any documents you need to as quickly as possible.

At this point in the loan process, three to four days have passed from the moment the contract was signed. Usually we are still waiting for the appraisal to come back (unless a rush fee has been paid), but we want to know by this point all of the conditions the underwriter has so we can make sure that all necessary documents are ready by the time the appraisal is ready. This ensures that the underwriter can sign off on your loan at one time, instead of reviewing everything piecemeal as it comes in.

The underwriting process usually takes about a week when using a standard thirty-day escrow. Once the appraisal and any other conditions are ready, everything is resubmitted to the underwriter, who will review everything within twenty-four to forty-eight hours. If everything is in shape, the underwriter will sign off on every condition, and you are clear to close. Clear to close means that there are no other conditions on your loan except for signing your closing disclosure and loan documents.

Remember, the closing disclosure will have all of the closing fees at their final amount, which is usually slightly less than the loan estimate disclosure you received earlier in the process. All of the fees on your closing disclosure will match to the penny what is on your final loan documents you sign on closing day.

Once you sign your closing disclosure, you have to wait three business days before you can sign your loan documents, a process the government implemented in 2015 to ensure that buyers and sellers understand what they are signing. Today, you will see your loan estimate and closing disclosure multiple times before you sign your final loan documents, so there is no question that you are fully aware of what you are agreeing to.

Being marked as clear to close also means you can release your loan contingency on the real estate side. At this point, all contingencies should be released and you are locked into the contract unless you are willing to give up your EMD.

LOAN DOCUMENTS

When you sign your loan documents, what you are signing is the note that states you are borrowing this amount of money for this number of years at this interest rate. This is the most important document you are going to sign in the inch-thick pile of papers you are given at closing. The note will explain what your interest rate is, the loan amount, your payments, and when the loan will be fully paid off (if you pay only the monthly payments at the agreed-upon amount).

The rest of the pages in the pile are disclosures specifying the fine print that attorneys have written for home purchasing. All of the loan documents for Fannie Mae, Freddie Mac, VA, FHA, and conventional loans are the same across every lending company because all lenders have to use the same fine print and guidelines. No changes can be made to these.

Once these documents are signed, it both is and isn't a binding contract.

When you are clear to close, that means there are no outstanding conditions on your loan. However, the escrow company still has to prove that you deposited your down payment in escrow. They cannot do that until you sign your loan documents, at which point escrow can order the wire transfer for funding. This is when your mortgage company will wire the funds to escrow to pay everything.

After everything is paid, proof of those payments along with the signed loan documents are sent to the underwriter, who can officially finish the loan and send it to be recorded. Your mortgage broker does not handle recording the title, however—the escrow company completes this part of the transaction.

One of your loan documents that you sign at closing is usually called the Grant Deed. This document states that the seller is granting the property to you because you paid them a certain amount of money. The escrow company takes the signed Grant Deed after it is notarized (done at closing) to the county recorder's office to be recorded. Once the escrow company has verification from the country recorder that the document is recorded, you become the legal owner of that property.

THE LOAN PROCESS IN DIFFERENT STATES

The loan process can differ slightly in some states. For instance, in California, which is an escrow state, once you sign your loan documents, there could be some additional conditions that you need to meet in order to finish the loan. You wouldn't be fully clear to close at that point.

Some states are attorney states, which means that you sit down at a table with the seller and everyone signs all the documents at the same time, the wire is requested while you are all in the room, the Grant Deed is recorded while you are in the room, and then you get handed your keys.

These differences mean that you may get your keys the day you sign your paperwork or you may get your keys in a few days. Your lender can and should walk you through what to expect based on where you are purchasing your property.

When done correctly, the loan process is very easy, especially if your lender has already fully underwritten pre-approved you. The goal of the loan process should be that it is so easy, you want to do it again—which you can if you want to buy additional real estate to increase your personal wealth with passive income.

CHAPTER NINE

How to Buy Additional Real Estate

In 2008, a close friend of mine and his wife, who worked for a local school system and had two children, had a property that was underwater. They had purchased their home in 2006, like many people, when home values were very high. Unfortunately, in 2008 when the market crashed, the value of most properties dropped drastically, and homeowners ended up having mortgages that were $100,000–$200,000 more than the property was now worth.

My friend and his wife needed help, so they came to me. I was able to help them sell that property quickly and purchase another property that was less money. However, at that time, you couldn't short sell a property because the property was underwater (when your loan is greater than the value of your property). You needed to prove hardship. I was able to help them prove hardship that prevented them from maintaining the property, so they were able to sell it and purchase a cheaper property—an older, three bedroom, two bath in Oak-dale, California.

Not long afterward, they came across another property that was coming up for sale for $80,000—an older two bedroom, one bath. They were able to snatch it up, and rent it out.

Their ultimate goal was to move to San Clemente, California—which is *the place* to live, located at the south end of Orange County, right before you pass into San Diego County—because they thought it would provide the best life for themselves and their children. Until then, they would vacation there every chance they had.

Eventually, they reached out to me and said, "We're ready to make the move. How can we do it with these two properties we currently own?"

On one of their trips, they had found a duplex that was located a block from the beach. It was unusual because duplexes are usually the same size on both sides, but this property consisted of three bedrooms and two baths on one side, and one bedroom and one bath on the other.

They knew they wanted to buy it but they weren't sure how. While they knew they could sell their other two properties and use those sales for the down payment, the profits wouldn't be enough for them to put down 25 percent on the new property. Instead of going that route, I was able to get them an FHA loan with a little finessing. FHA loans, along with conventional loans, have a max amount for a two-unit property. At the time, the max for San Clemente was set at $840,000, and the property they wanted to purchase cost $950,000, so they needed to be able to pay $110,000 out of pocket. While that may sound like a lot, in reality, using FHA allowed them to put less than 12 percent down on the property. If they had used a conventional loan, they would have needed to put 20 to 25 percent down, which would have been $190,000–$240,000.

The couple was able to sell both of their properties, which gave them enough to purchase the new property in their dream location. When selling the smaller property, the appraisal was coming in at $10,000 less than what my friend wanted to sell it for. At first, he was upset. He didn't want to lose out on $10,000. I told him, "Don't step over a dollar to pick up a dime. The beach property will increase in value by at least $100,000 the first year because it's a block from the beach, and no one is building that close anymore."

He decided to let the $10,000 go, and to this day, he gives other people the same advice: don't step over a dollar to pick up a dime. His beach property did increase that first year from $950,000 to $1,040,000. He made $90,000 by selling one property for $10,000 less than he had hoped for. Fast-forward five years later, their property is worth over $2 million and they have been able to rent the one-bed, one-bath side of the duplex as an Airbnb since the day he and his family moved in, which brings them in anywhere from $3,000–$5,000 a month. That income pays for their mortgage and allows them to remodel their side of the property.

Today, they still live in that duplex, a block from the beach, working as a principal and a school social worker, and have a million dollars in equity in the home, an amount they never would have made in such a short time with their jobs. Their kids are constantly surfing every chance they get—which is a lot of chances when the waves are a two-minute walk away.

When you plan right with real estate, you can create your dream life.

MAKING A FORTUNE IN REAL ESTATE

Most wealthy people today made their fortune thanks to real estate. During the 2008 downturn, they purchased properties that were at historically low prices, well under their actual value, and then rented them out to the people who had wanted to buy the home but were unable to due to a loss of income or savings (because of the same downturn that made others rich). Today, we're seeing the same thing happen, which is causing a problem for people who want to purchase a home.

Many building companies and corporations are currently building single-family home tracks for rent only because it is so lucrative to be a landlord today. (Again, think of Pottersville from *It's a Wonderful Life*.) Many millennials don't want to live in an apartment, especially after the COVID pandemic, and they don't want to own a house, but they want a yard and space.

Historically, it used to be that everyone would buy a duplex, triplex, or fourplex, and then rent it out to make passive income, which makes sense. When you're looking to buy real estate for income, the best way to build your portfolio is to buy a triplex or fourplex, live in one unit, clean up the other units as needed, rent them out, and then buy your own single-family home. You can move into that home (letting you rent out your old unit), and after you live there for a while, follow the same process: buy a new home and rent out the old home. And then do it again. This enables you to build your portfolio over time with the least amount of money down.

If you purchase something as an investment property without plans to live in it, you have to put a minimum of 20 percent down, but to get the best rate, you need to put at least 25 percent down. However, if you are purchasing property and you plan to live in one unit, you can put down as little as 3.5 percent.

Say the property in question is $300,000. You would only need $10,500 for 3.5 percent down versus $75,000 for 25 percent, which leaves a lot more money in your pocket.

The key is to pay attention to your loan statements. Typically, the loan documents will state that you must live on the property as your primary residence for at least one year. After a year, you can move out and have your renters pay for the entire mortgage. The moment your renters' total rent increases over the mortgage payment amount, you begin to receive passive income.

So, not only do you receive passive income once you move out and rent exceeds the payment, but you still have the difference you would have paid had you not lived in the house because you decided to live there for a year. Now, at the end of the year, you have money in the bank to purchase another property.

This is the cheapest and easiest way to get into real estate and begin earning long-term passive income, especially when you retire. Most people don't have enough savings for retirement, but if you follow this pattern over a period of thirty years, you'll reach a point where all the money for rent is now income with no mortgage to consider. If you are starting this process later in life, it can still work for you—you just won't receive all of the income from it in fifteen years.

At one point in time, it was popular for people later in life to borrow money from their 401k to purchase real estate and generate passive income. Today, profit sharing is more popular. You buy real estate with, and as a part of, your retirement portfolio, and then, if you ever sell it, that profit goes back into your retirement account.

The key is that there are many ways to acquire property for passive income. However, don't be in a hurry to get several properties quickly. It's about doing it over time, like purchasing stocks. Dollar cost averaging is more effective because values of properties go up and down similarly to stocks. Therefore, the values average out when purchased over time. Essentially, what you are doing is adding better value to your investments.

Plus, you can always refinance your properties during a time when there is a decrease in interest rates. Many people in mid-2022 are worried about purchasing property because of a recent increase in rates. However, rates go up and down constantly over the years, so they shouldn't affect your decision to purchase. In fact, you'll have less competition for your dream home when rates are higher.

THE QUALIFICATIONS TO PURCHASE MULTIPLE PROPERTIES

Let's say you want to purchase a single-family home to move into, so you can leave the duplex that was your first property.

To offset the mortgage on your first property, your lender can use 75 percent of the income from the property.

For example, if you are renting your duplex for $3,000 a month, you can use $2,250 of that rent to offset the mortgage on that property. If the mortgage of the duplex is $2,500, you will be negative $250 a month, which is debt the lender has to count against you when you go to purchase your new property. It would be classified the same as having credit card debt or a car loan payment of $250 a month.

The reason lenders can only use 75 percent of the rent is because they are assuming a vacancy factor of a quarter, meaning they are assuming that a quarter of the time, that property will not be rented.

For situations where you are buying your first rental property and you are putting 25 percent down, your lender can also take 75 percent of the rent that you will make and use that to offset the mortgage.

PROGRAMS TO PURCHASE ADDITIONAL REAL ESTATE

The one constant when it comes to the programs available to purchase additional real estate is that the available programs change constantly.

At the time of writing, you can get 25-percent-down conventional programs through Fannie Mae and Freddie Mac. However, Fannie and Freddy don't want to approve too many rental programs, because a lot of investors purchased additional real estate to rent during the pandemic when the rates were at their lowest, and both lending companies are now over-leveraged with rental mortgages.

While conventional may not be the way to go, there are also programs called DSCR, which is a debt service type of loan. Each DSCR program has its own ratio that changes often, but for example, say you are buying a duplex that has a mortgage of $2,000 a month and you have enough rent to offset that payment, so you will need to get $2,500 in rent, which is a 1.25 percent DSCR. These programs use only the property value and the rent of the property when considering the loan, instead of you and your income.

To find out which loan program is best for your second property needs, talk to your mortgage broker. The loan space is constantly changing due to current rates, law, policy initiatives, and market variability, so it's best to work with someone whose full-time job is to stay on top of this information. If you don't have a mortgage broker you trust, send me an email at ask@ edparcaut.com and I can send you a list of what programs are currently available.

MANAGING RENTAL PROPERTIES

There are two ways to manage rental properties.

1. Handle the property management yourself (you rent the units out, you are their credit, you handle any issues that come up).
2. Find a property management company to handle it for you.

I always recommend the second option. On average, the property management company will take 10 percent of the rent, but they guarantee your renter. If you need to do an eviction, they handle that. It also makes more sense over time as you build up your portfolio of properties.

Managing a property means handling rent collection (and following up on it if it's late), eviction, finding new renters, and property maintenance. If you are purchasing a rental property, the first thing you need to buy is a home warranty on that property, whether you are going to live there or not. Ensure that you use a reputable home warranty company (again, email me for a current list of companies).

When I was renting a property, I had a renter call because their garbage disposal wasn't working. I was able to call the home warranty company, pay the service call fee of $75, and they contacted the renter to make an appointment and replace the disposal. It was extremely easy for both me and the renter. I didn't have to make the repairs myself or find a handyman, and the renter didn't have to wait a long time for me to do either of those things.

By using a property management company in combination with a home warranty, every aspect of renting is handled for you, making it a hands-off way to gain passive income. Plus, it makes it easier for you to have a rental property in California even if you move to Pennsylvania. For the convenience, the company will take an average of 10 percent off the top of your rent income. Keep in mind that you will need to put the rent you receive on your tax return, so by having the management company take 10 percent off the rent, it works essentially as a deduction, which can reduce your tax bill while also saving you a great deal of hassle.

A note on moving states: if you are moving to another state, consider renting out your property instead of selling it, in case you don't want to live in the new state forever. I've had clients sell their house in California, move to another state, and when they wanted to move back, found that they couldn't afford to buy there anymore. They had been priced out—and some of them priced out in only a year because of a high period of appreciation while they were gone.

WHEN YOU SHOULDN'T PURCHASE AN ADDITIONAL PROPERTY

Whether or not you should purchase additional property will depend on your life plan. If you're successful with your business and sell it for several million dollars, you may not need passive income from real estate—but you could use that money to put into real estate for additional income.

I honestly believe it is always a good idea to buy real estate. However, for most people who haven't sold a business for a seven-figure profit, you should purchase real estate over time. Before you purchase another property, you need to make sure that you can cover the costs of that transaction (down payment, closing costs, etc.) and that you are making enough money and rent to offset the additional mortgage payment. I've seen too many people try to purchase a second property when they are –$500 a month in payments and end up losing both properties. If you can't, it may not be the right time or the right property for you.

As long as you can purchase the property and not hurt yourself financially, I believe you should invest in a second or third property—over time—for long-term passive income. I've said it multiple times because it's important: you need to purchase over time, because if you buy too many properties at once, you can lose all of them.

One of my new clients told me a story about losing three properties in Arizona, one in Tennessee, and one in California because he bought them too close together and with the wrong loan programs. He had purchased most of them with 100 percent financing. The first mortgage had a fixed rate that turned into an adjustable rate over time with a 6 percent margin on it, meaning that the lender added the interest to the back end of the mortgage.

Unfortunately, during the downturn, a lot of people moved back in with family because they had lost their jobs and couldn't afford to pay rent anymore. Therefore, a lot of units became available for rent with no one to rent them. The few renters paid less than what my client owed for the mortgage payments. Over time, while covering the gap between the rental payment and the mortgage payment, my client ran out of money. He couldn't make the mortgage payments anymore and lost the properties.

Purchase over time so you can be sure that you are cash flow-positive with each additional property. Renting out properties is a great way to earn long-term passive income and begin to increase your personal wealth, as long as it's done correctly.

Conclusion

Throughout this book, I've shown you that even if you think there's a bubble coming or interest rates are increasing, now is still the time to purchase your first home.

Look at the number of homes that are currently being built. At the time of writing (June 2022), we are on schedule to build 1.7 million homes and 1.4 million household creations, which means people coming of age and starting a family, annualized year over year. That leaves 300,000 extra homes. However, about 100,000 homes are lost due to age and disaster every year.

That only leaves 200,000 homes across the country to help address the home shortage that buyers are experiencing right now. Fannie Mae states that if we continue on this trend—200,000 additional homes over need built a year—it will take nineteen years to catch up to the amount of homes needed. (If you're doing the math, that's 4.3 million homes needed, according to Fannie and Freddie.)

The importance of this number is that, no matter what market you're looking at while reading this book, we are still in a position to make it the perfect time to buy a home (unless it's been twenty years since publication, and in that case, you should email me about current market conditions). In the next twenty years, you are not going to run into a situation like the Great Recession where your home value will drop underneath what your home is worth. Demand is high and supply is low, so home value and prices are going to continue to rise.

Even if you purchase a home and decide to sell two years later, you won't lose money on the sale because of the current home shortage and supply chain issues.

Once you've decided to purchase your home, it's important to understand your credit score. In fact, it's the most important thing to understand. You need to know what your current score is and how to get to the right score if yours is low. If your score is over 760, you don't need to worry about it, but anything less, you should review it and work to improve it.

Another factor to review before purchase is your income and budget. Remember, it's not always about what you can qualify for. I've qualified clients for a $4,000-a-month mortgage payment who don't want that high of a payment, regardless of what the debt-to-income ratio model says they can afford. Instead, they want a lower payment because they created a monthly budget and knew that a $4,000 payment would result in living outside their means.

However, if the payment for the house you want is a $200 to $300-a-month difference, you can make some lifestyle changes and adjust your budget to be able to afford it. Maybe you can purchase an espresso machine for the new house instead of going to Starbucks five days a week, which is easily a $150-a-month habit. Or you could stop eating out for lunch and dinner every day. Allocate the same amount of money to different areas of your budget so that you can afford the house you want, without going over what you can afford.

When your mortgage broker tells you what you qualify for, don't think you need to use that amount. Choose an amount that works for your situation in life now. Don't use the max amount and then be house-poor, unable to do anything you want because you purchased an expensive house. Know your budget and work within it.

If you want a more expensive house and it doesn't work in your current budget, look for a better job or ask for a raise. At time of writing, there were 11 million jobs available. Remember the gentleman who tried to qualify using his overtime in Chapter 2? He wasn't able to use that overtime as part of his income because he hadn't received it for two years so he was unable to qualify for the house he wanted.

Two years later, he came back to me and he can now use that overtime as part of his income. Unfortunately, interest rates have increased, so he once again couldn't qualify for the house. The good news is that he has not received a raise in those two years, so he was able to go to his boss and ask for the raise. They gave it to him and the additional two dollars an hour was all he needed to qualify for and purchase the home.

Even if you don't qualify for the home you want at the moment, you can either get a better job or see if you are due for a raise. A few dollars more an hour can be the difference in qualification.

In the beginning of 2020, almost everyone qualified to purchase a home, but there were not enough homes available. Today, the same number of homes are on the market but not enough people are qualifying due to the interest increase. For sellers, this means that instead of twenty people writing offers, only five people are writing offers. This is great for buyers, because it gives you a better chance to get the house you want.

When you are signing a contract for offer or an acceptance of your offer—any contract during the process—make sure you review it carefully. Check all of the dates on it and be sure you can meet them. Identify any contingencies and their respective release dates. This is a legally binding contract, so understand what you are signing. Don't sign it because your agent tells you to. Don't sign disclosures because your mortgage broker assures you they're right. You need to read every page of what you are signing. This is why you are provided the same loan documents over and over—so you have plenty of time to read and understand them.

If you're getting your first home, I strongly urge you to look at buying a multi-unit property before a single-family home, especially if you are young. I was recently at a live event with a real estate agent who told me how surprised he was when two young people shadowing him for the day talked about the fact that their first home should be a duplex or triplex. They knew that they could buy it for 3.5 percent down with an FHA loan, as it was their first property, use the rent to help them qualify for the price, and start building their personal wealth and passive income. Once you have a single-family home, it's difficult to go into the unit business without 20 to 25 percent down.

YOUR NEXT STEPS

Now that you understand the homebuying process, it's time to go buy your first home.

If you have further questions about the process or you don't know which mortgage broker or realtor to use in your area, please reach out to me at ask@edparcaut.com and I'll refer you to someone.

It's important that you start the homebuying process as soon as possible because the best way to build personal wealth is through home ownership.

Acknowledgments

I want to thank my wife, the most important person in my life. She supports me in all my endeavors in life. Without her smile, I would not have been able to write this book or be on the radio and host multiple podcasts.

I want to thank my children Alexis, Roshea, Sydney, and Blake for making me want to leave knowledge so they will have the opportunity to build personal wealth.

I want to thank the whole Scribe team; without them this book would never have happened.